New Private Monies

A Bit-Part Player?

New Private Monies

A Bit-Part Player?

KEVIN DOWD

The Institute of Economic Affairs

First published in Great Britain in 2014 by
The Institute of Economic Affairs
2 Lord North Street
Westminster
London SW1P 3LB
in association with the Cobden Centre
www.cobdencentre.org
and London Publishing Partnership Ltd
www.londonpublishingpartnership.co.uk

The mission of the Institute of Economic Affairs is to improve public understanding of the fundamental institutions of a free society, with particular reference to the role of markets in solving economic and social problems.

A CIP catalogue record for this book is available from the British Library.

ISBN 978-0-255-36694-6

Many IEA publications are translated into languages other than English or are reprinted. Permission to translate or to reprint should be sought from the Director General at the address above.

Typeset in Kepler by T&T Productions Ltd
www.tandtproductions.com

Printed and bound in Great Britain by Page Bros

CONTENTS

THE AUTHOR

Kevin Dowd is professor of finance and economics at Durham University and a partner in Cobden Partners. A lifelong classical liberal, his main interests are in private money and free banking, but he is also interested in general political economy, monetary and financial economics, regulation, risk management and pensions. His books include *Private Money: The Path to Monetary Stability* (IEA, 1998); *The State and the Monetary System* (Philip Allan, 1989); *Laissez-Faire Banking* (Routledge, 1992); *Competition and Finance: A New Interpretation of Financial and Monetary Economics* (Macmillan, 1996); and, most recently, with Martin Hutchinson, *Alchemists of Loss: How Modern Finance and Government Intervention Crashed the Financial System* (Wiley, 2010). He edited *The Experience of Free Banking* (Routledge, 1992) and (with R. H. Timberlake, Jr) *Money and the Nation State: The Financial Revolution, Government and the World Monetary System* (Transaction Publishers, 1998). He has published widely in academic journals and is an adjunct scholar of the Cato Institute, a senior fellow with the Cobden Centre and a member of the Academic Advisory Council of the Institute of Economic Affairs. He lives in Sheffield, England, with his family.

FOREWORD

In the 2014 Budget, the Chancellor of the Exchequer, George Osborne, announced that a new pound coin would be issued. The Chancellor made much of the fact that it would have twelve sides and look like the old 'three-penny bit'. It was interesting that the Chancellor chose to make such a comparison. When the new coin is brought in it will buy just 20 per cent more than the three-penny bit bought when it was introduced to replace the silver three pence coin in 1937. This illustrates the poor record of state money when it comes to keeping its purchasing power and maintaining a store of value.

State monies have increasingly become open to competition with each other as a result of the breakdown of exchange controls. Arguably, this has been one of the factors that has led to better inflation performance. However, there has been very little competition between state money and private sector monies. Now, that situation is changing – though only at the margin.

Kevin Dowd, one of the foremost experts on private money and free banking, takes us through the recent history of private monetary systems. Some of these have been based on gold, such as the Liberty Dollar and e-gold; others, such as Bitcoin, have been based on an entirely new system of limiting supply.

Many questions remain about the potential of these new innovations. For example, will they be able to fulfil the functions of money by becoming generally acceptable and maintaining a store of value? Will they reach a point where acceptability is sufficiently widespread that the network economies that we expect of money can be realised? Kevin Dowd does not pretend he knows the answers to these questions with certainty. However, he is sceptical that the new private monies of which we are currently aware will be the innovation that ends the state money monopoly. Nevertheless, new developments in this field have the potential to develop in such a way that they are able to transcend state money in ways that we cannot currently foresee. We need a process of competition to ensure that, should such new developments be beneficial, they will thrive.

It is doubtful that the environment exists currently that is conducive to such a process of competition. Law enforcement agencies have clamped down on new private monies and the regulatory environment in the US seems especially problematic. It is worth noting that many of the users of private monies see themselves as purposefully trying to undermine the regulatory power of an ever-more intrusive state. It is not surprising that the state objects to this.

Private monies have been used for certain illicit purposes and this is an issue on which readers will have different views – they may also differ on whether certain types of transaction should or should not be illegal. However, there are many ways in which people can evade the law and it is incumbent on law enforcement authorities to tackle evasion of the law explicitly rather than through trying to stamp out innovation within monetary systems and competition between them. Private monies are also used by people who simply wish to 'thumb their nose' at the state without doing anything illegal. They should feel at liberty to do this.

As with any other economic development, we cannot predict the future of new private monies with any accuracy. Nevertheless, Kevin Dowd performs a great service by helping readers obtain a better understanding of the likely prospects of success. If the state had still controlled telephony and banned all competition with fixed-line telephony, would we have had the iPhone and its competitors today? It is very doubtful to say the least. As such, it is important that the state leaves open the door to currency competition so that innovation is not choked off. Such innovations may take years or decades and many will fail, but we need to allow people to harness valuable innovation as it happens. As the author reminds us, this suggests that the government would do well to leave private monies alone.

The IEA commends this monograph to all who are interested in the future of money and, indeed, to all who are interested in the process of innovation in a free economy more generally.

PHILIP BOOTH
Editorial and Programme Director
Institute of Economic Affairs
Professor of Insurance and Risk Management
Cass Business School, City University

April 2014

The views expressed in this monograph are, as in all IEA publications, those of the author and not those of the Institute (which has no corporate view), its managing trustees, Academic Advisory Council members or senior staff. With some exceptions, such as with the publication of lectures, all IEA monographs are blind peer reviewed by at least two academics or researchers who are experts in the field.

ACKNOWLEDGEMENTS

This monograph is a much revised version of an earlier draft prepared for the Liberty Fund Conference, 'In Search of a Monetary Constitution Revisited', 19–22 April 2012, in Freiburg, Germany. I thank Viktor Vanberg, Lawrence H. White and the Liberty Fund for the invitation to participate in this conference, and I thank Steve Baker MP, Maneck Bodhanwala, Dave Campbell, Martin Hutchinson, Doug Jackson, Gordon Kerr, Duncan Kitchin, Matthias Klaes, Bernard von NotHaus, Frederick Roeder, Lawrence H. White, Basil Zafiriou and two referees for many helpful inputs that have much improved the draft. The usual caveat applies.

SUMMARY

- A private money is a widely accepted medium of exchange or payment issued by a non-governmental body in the absence of any legal privileges. Private monies do not have to be generally acceptable; they merely have to be widely accepted. Three examples of contemporary private monetary systems are the Liberty Dollar, e-gold and cryptocurrencies. The former two are based on precious metals and the best-known instance of the latter is Bitcoin.
- There is a public demand for and interest in private currencies from various groups of people. Some wish to hold private currencies in the expectation that they will not diminish in purchasing power as state money has; some wish to conduct illegal activity; some wish to be part of a movement against increasing state control of economic and personal behaviour; and others just want better money.
- The Liberty Dollar was based on a private mint that issued gold and silver coins; it also issued notes redeemable in precious metals. It was periodically revalued against the US dollar as the value of the latter fell over time against the precious metals. The Liberty Dollar was specifically designed to function in parallel with and in competition to the US dollar and never marketed or represented as official US currency.

- The Liberty Dollar was highly successful and became the second most popular currency in the US. Though initially tolerated, the US government turned against the Liberty Dollar, declared its use a federal crime and eventually secured a conviction against its founder for counterfeiting, fraud and conspiracy against the United States. This was an extraordinary result given that the purpose of the founders of the Liberty Dollar was to produce a currency that was distinct from but superior to the greenback dollar, and there was never any attempt to pass off the former for the latter.

- e-gold was a private digital gold currency, a digital payment system in which the unit of account is gold and in which user accounts are backed by gold reserves. It was an 'offshore' payment system rather than a money transmitter or bank as defined under then-existing regulations, not least because gold was not legally 'money'. By 2005, e-gold had grown to be second only to PayPal in the online payments industry: it had 1.2 million accounts and transactions that year totalled $1.5 billion.

- US law enforcement services also turned on e-gold and its principals were indicted in April 2007. The charges boiled down to e-gold being an unlicensed money-transmitting entity and a means of moving the proceeds of illegal activities with the principals' tacit knowledge. These charges were never proven and even the judge in the e-gold case expressed major doubts about the government case.

- Bitcoin is a totally decentralised monetary system that would be very difficult for the law enforcement agencies to shut down because it has no single 'point of failure'. Bitcoin is produced by a 'digital mining' process that is intended to limit its supply in a way that is in some ways analogous to the supply process of gold under a gold standard. As with other cryptocurrencies, Bitcoin has the potential to restore financial privacy and create a peaceful crypto-anarchic social order that operates beyond government control.

- The demand for Bitcoin has taken off since its launch in 2009 and it is increasingly used for both legal and illegal transactions, the latter thanks to its potential to achieve a very high degree of transactions anonymity. These illegal transactions include, most notoriously, its use to trade illegal drugs on the Silk Road dark web marketplace.

- Though the supply of Bitcoin is limited, the demand is very variable; this variability has made its price very uncertain and created a bubble–bust cycle in the Bitcoin market. Perhaps the safest prediction is that Bitcoin will eventually be displaced by alternative cryptocurrencies with superior features.

- The appropriate government response to private money is to allow competition on a level playing field between alternative forms of money. As with the provision of other goods and services, competition would best promote good money and drive out bad.

FIGURES

1   INTRODUCTION

This monograph examines contemporary private, or nongovernmental, monetary systems. At one level, mention of a private monetary system has still not lost its capacity to shock: it raises connotations of individuals printing their own banknotes and putting them into circulation, or even minting their own coins. Yet, at another level, privately issued money is familiar and commonplace, and all kinds of private money already circulate widely. Examples include gift certificates, grocery store vouchers and Chuck E. Cheese tokens. Bank deposits are another example. In fact, most of the outstanding money in circulation is privately issued. However, my focus of interest is not on these familiar, sometimes regulated and frankly boring forms of private money but rather with unregulated or loosely regulated varieties of private money that emerge spontaneously via market forces and operate outside government control: individuals printing their own currency or minting their own coins are perfect examples.

Most private monetary systems consist of local paper currency or credit systems such as local economic trading systems (LETS), community mutual credit systems, time banks, local paper currency and company scrip, which was often issued as a means of payment when regular currency was unavailable, such as in remote mining towns or on long voyages.[1] They also include local private bank currency, such as the clearing house loan certificates and other forms of private emergency currency issued by US banks in the period before the founding of the Federal Reserve.[2] Well-known contemporary examples in the US include Potomacs, Ithaca Hours and BerkShares. Innumerable instances of these systems have been recorded over the years, and one would imagine that there must be many thousands of them operating in the US today. In fact, there are so many across the world that there is even a research journal devoted to them, the *International Journal of Community Currency Research*.[3] A second form of private money is private coinage, which also has a long and successful – not to mention, colourful – history.[4]

The subject of private money raises an important definitional issue: what exactly *is* private money? In this monograph, the term is used to refer to a widely accepted medium of exchange or payment issued by a non-governmental body in the absence of any legal privileges. The term '*widely* accepted medium of exchange' is used rather than the more standard definition of a '*generally* accepted medium of exchange' because no private money – apart

---

1   Timberlake (1987) provides a classic study on private scrip money.

2   Again, Timberlake provides the definitive study: Timberlake (1984).

3   http://www.ijccr.net.

4   There are many studies of private coinage. Examples include those by Brough (1898), Barnard (1917) and, more recently, Selgin (2008).

from bank deposits which often are backed by some form of legal privilege or guarantee – can be regarded as generally accepted.

This working definition also requires that the money in question is not just issued by a non-governmental body – after all, the Federal Reserve is technically a private organisation, as was the Bank of England until 1946. The money must also be issued in the absence of legal privilege or state guarantees. The latter qualifier rules out Federal Reserve currency as private money. We can therefore think of private money as generally operating on the fringes (at least) of the official monetary system, competing with official money, although some private monies have the potential to displace official money altogether.

A persistent and complex theme of historical private money systems is their often uneasy relationship with the state. The state has typically had a dual role towards them. In most cases it has been a destroyer. But, in other cases, it has been a creator of sorts, or at least an unwitting midwife. On the one hand, the typical response of the state has been to stamp out private money. The usual motive was the obvious one: private monetary systems were often seen as a threat to the ability of the state to raise seignorage and an affront to the prerogatives of the state itself. On the other hand, though the state never set out to do so, it was often the state that enabled these private monetary systems by creating the circumstances that led them to emerge in the first place. The system of clearing house loan certificates mentioned earlier is a good example: this was a direct consequence of the note issue restrictions of the National

Banking System legislation of the 1860s. Another example is the bills of exchange system in early nineteenth-century Lancashire: this arose to fill a gap created by the refusal of the Bank of England to service the area properly combined with the legal inability of other banks to do so (see, for example, Baxendale 2011). In these and many other cases, private money emerged to fill a market niche that the state itself had created.

This monograph focuses on three contemporary (and predominantly US) cases of private monetary systems that have received a lot of recent publicity:

- The Liberty Dollar: this is a dollar-denominated gold- and silver-based monetary system that can function in an environment where the values of the precious metals have fluctuated greatly against the dollar.
- Digital Gold Currency (DGC) with the focus on the best-known such system, e-gold: these are gold-based payments systems that proved to be particularly useful for international payments.
- Bitcoin: this is the first successful example of the most recent form of private currency, cryptocurrency, and is path-breaking in a number of ways. It is a radical new type of currency based on the principles of strong cryptography; it has a novel production process – a form of digital 'mining' for want of a better description – that we have never seen before; it offers users the potential for anonymous and untraceable transactions; it runs itself and is the first ever private monetary system that is completely decentralised;

it is not so much unregulated as 'unregulatable' and it apparently cannot be shut down. Bitcoin is truly revolutionary.

As with their historical predecessors, all three cases illustrate that the US government still remains hostile to private money. Though both the Liberty Dollar and e-gold prove that there is a strong public demand for gold-based private money and were successful in providing it, they were attacked by the government and, after highly questionable legal processes, their founders were convicted of criminal activities and their operations closed down. One can safely infer that the government would even more readily attack Bitcoin if it could, but it currently lacks the means to do so. Whereas the Liberty Dollar and e-gold were produced by identifiable individuals that the government could apprehend, Bitcoin is an altogether different proposition: it is an apparently unbreakable cryptocurrency issued by an anonymous user network, widely used on anonymous hidden exchanges that the government cannot locate. It was promoted and designed by cyber (or, should I say, cypher) anarchists who openly aspire to shut down the government itself. The issues raised by contemporary private monetary systems are, thus, far-reaching.

This monograph is organised as follows. Chapter 2 examines the Liberty Dollar and Chapter 3 examines digital currency, with the emphasis on DGC systems and the case of e-gold. Chapter 4 describes Bitcoin and other cryptocurrencies and then Chapter 5 discusses one of the most remarkable features of cryptocurrencies: their ability to protect individuals' financial privacy and the profound implications that follow from that. It means, for example, that people are able to operate beyond government control and there are, of course, ensuing issues that are raised by a newly emerging anarchic social order. Chapter 6 concludes.

2 THE LIBERTY DOLLAR

The Liberty Dollar was designed by Bernard von NotHaus, the founder of the National Organization for the Repeal of the Federal Reserve and the Internal Revenue Code (NORFED). It was launched on 1 October 1998. At its inception, von NotHaus announced that his objective was to 'be to the Federal Reserve System what Federal Express was to the Post Office' by providing a private voluntary barter currency as an alternative to Federal Reserve currency. The new Liberty Dollar was to be based primarily on gold and silver coinage – though strictly speaking they should be described in law as 'medallions'[1] – and its precious metallic basis was to provide protection against the inflation

---

1   In private correspondence, Mr von NotHaus informs me that the Liberty Dollar organisation was always extremely careful never to refer to any of its specie pieces as a coin because issuing coins for monetary purposes in the US would have been in violation of 18 USC §486, which states:

> Whoever, except as authorized by law, makes or utters or passes, or attempts to utter or pass, any coins of gold or silver or other metal, or alloys of metals, intended for use as current money, whether in the resemblance of coins of the United States or of foreign countries, or of original design, shall be fined under this title or imprisoned not more than five years, or both.

to which the inconvertible dollar has been prone since World War II, thanks to the Federal Reserve's predilection for expansionist monetary policies.

The Liberty Dollar consists primarily of coins in gold and silver; a second component consisted of warehouse receipts redeemable on demand in specie stored securely in an audited warehouse in Idaho; and a third component, the 'eLibertyDollar', consisted of digital warehouse receipts.[2] Thus, the Liberty Dollar existed in specie, paper and digital form, and all forms of the Liberty Dollar were denominated in units of Liberty Dollars.

Trading Liberty Dollars for greenbacks

The designers of the Liberty Dollar faced a major technical problem: how could the Liberty Dollar trade at par against the US government dollar, the greenback, when the value of the Liberty Dollar is based on the values of the precious metals, but the value of the US dollar depends on Federal

---

I shall therefore use his terminology for reasons of legal precision, but readers are free to interpret the terms 'coin' and 'medallion' interchangeably if they wish.

2   The digital version of the Liberty Dollar was launched in November 2002 and users could email digital Liberty Dollars to each other or use them in online trade. The system was highly secure, audited monthly and charges were very low (zero for transactions under $10 and 37 cents for other transactions) and much lower than was being charged, for example, by Visa or Mastercard. This system was highly successful and a large amount of the Liberty Dollar gold and silver that was eventually confiscated by the government in 2009 backed the digital warehouse receipts.

Reserve monetary policy? The way in which the Liberty Dollar handled this problem is very interesting.

Consider that a silver Liberty Dollar medallion with a face value of $10 was minted in 1998 with an ounce of silver at a time when the current market price of silver was about $5 an ounce. The difference between the $10 face value and the $5 cost of the silver input covered costs of production and any minter's profit, and the medallion itself would be sold for $10 or $7.50 to distributors. Other things being equal, if the market price of silver then remained below $7.50 an ounce, the organisation could continue to mint such medallions indefinitely – and it would keep retailing them for $10, which means that the Liberty Dollar and the US dollar would trade at par, one dollar for the other.

However, if the US dollar price of silver rises – due in the long run to expansionary monetary policy by the Federal Reserve – the profit from minting falls and there comes a point – before the silver price hits $7.50 – beyond which it is no longer economic to continue minting Liberty Dollars. So, if the Liberty Dollar organisation continued to mint such medallions, it would eventually be bankrupted. If the price of silver were then to rise beyond $10, the Liberty Dollar medallions with a face value of ten dollars would have a silver content worth more than $10 and their price against the US dollar would rise: i.e. the Liberty Dollar medallion with a face value of $10 would trade for more than $10.

To forestall such an outcome and maintain parity against the US dollar, once the price of silver hit $7.50, the standard one-ounce silver Liberty Dollar was rebased upwards to have a face value of $20. This entailed the following:

- The Liberty Dollar organisation would now issue one-ounce silver medallions with a face value of $20 rather than a face value of $10 as before, and these were sold for $20 (note that this means that the new $20 Liberty Dollar medallions had the same metallic content as the old $10 Liberty medallions).
- Any holders of the old $10 face value one-ounce silver medallions would be entitled to exchange them for the new one-ounce silver medallions with a face value of $20, since the two have the same content.

The net result is that the Liberty Dollar would remain trading at par[3] against the US dollar and, in the process, people holding Liberty Dollars would have doubled the value of their holdings against the greenback. As von NotHaus explained:

---

3 Strictly speaking, it would be more accurate to say that 'in print' or newly minted $20 one-ounce silver Liberty Dollars would now be trading for $20. However, the older 'out of print' $10 one-ounce silver Liberty Dollars would now trade at a new price – approximately US$20 – reflecting the rights of their owners to trade them in for the new $20 silver Liberty Dollars which are now selling at $20. Speaking more generally, since they are also collectibles, the prices of out-of-print issues are also affected by how many of any particular issue are available and the scarcer issues would trade at a premium. Indeed, some were trading on eBay at very considerable prices before the government banned eBay from trading Liberty Dollars on the grounds that they were counterfeit currency.

The first move up (rebasement) was a big WOW for the Liberty Dollar as the currency actually moved up [against the greenback] as the model called for. And when it did, DOUBLE WOW ... people rushed to exchange their $10 Silver Libertys for new $20 Silver Libertys and double their money ... it was a smashing success.[4]

Liberty Dollar notes

The paper certificates had Liberty Dollar face values of $1, $5 and $10 that were claims for a specific amount of silver. For example, early certificates contemporary with the $10 one-ounce silver Liberty medallion would have a face value of $10 and entitle the holder to redeem one ounce of 0.999 fine silver from the organisation's warehouse. These certificates were not notes akin to those of a silver- or gold-standard bank operating on a fractional reserve, but were actually warehouse receipts backed by a 100 per cent reserve of silver. However, when the medallions were re-based, certificate holders could trade their old $10 certificates for new certificates with the new face value: for example, when the one-ounce silver $10 Liberty was rebased to a one-ounce $20 silver Liberty, the holder of one-ounce silver certificates with a face value of $10 was invited to exchange them for one-ounce silver certificates with a face value of $20, redeem it for silver or hold it for future rebasements. Holders of eLibertyDollar, the digital equivalent, could have their holdings rebased in the same way. These arrangements protected holders' silver and gold content

---

4   Personal correspondence.

claims and meant that the face values of their certificates or digital holdings over time kept roughly in sync with the values of the precious metals.

The Liberty Dollar in exchange and as a store of value

The Liberty Dollar was specifically designed to function in parallel with the US dollar and never marketed or represented as official US currency. Indeed, its whole marketing campaign was based precisely on the fact that it was *not* US official currency but, rather, superior to it.[5]

The Liberty Dollar was backed up by a persuasive marketing pitch. To quote from one of its brochures:

> Now you have a clear choice of money. Are you ready to grow and protect your money or will you continue to lose your purchasing power as the US dollar depreciates?
>
> Just as FedEx brought choice to the US Post Office, the Liberty Dollar brings choice to the US dollar and protection for your purchasing power.
>
> The Liberty Dollar is 100% inflation proof. It is real gold and silver that you can use just like cash where it is

---

5 The Liberty Dollar company went to great lengths to distinguish itself from official US coinage. As we have seen, they scrupulously avoided using the term 'coin', but they also avoided the term 'legal tender': to quote one of their statements, '[t]he Liberty Dollar has *never* claimed to be, does *not* claim to be, is *not*, and does *not* purport to be, legal tender.' Instead, the company saw the Liberty Dollar as a form of barter – their preferred wording was 'private voluntary barter currency' – which people could use for exchange if they wished to.

accepted voluntarily for everyday purchases at your grocery store, dentist or gas station...

When you are paying, ask the cashier, 'Would you
like plastic, paper or Silver?' Then reach out and drop
the Liberty Dollar in the cashier's hand. Join the fun by
simply offering the Liberty Dollar for all your goods and
services.

The Liberty Dollar was highly successful and became
the second most popular currency in the US. From 1998 to
2007, Liberty Dollar issues totalled up to perhaps $85m in
value. Over this same period, the company issued over 350
different specimens in paper or gold, silver, platinum or
copper specie that were distributed to around 250,000 customers. The Liberty Dollar was also accepted as a means
of exchange. Indeed, while von NotHaus encouraged sup-
porters to use the Liberty Dollar at 'mom and pop' mer-
chants, one supporter produced a list of all the major brand
names that had accepted it. The company that accepted it
most was Walmart, where it was used in hundreds of their
stores.[6]

Since the Liberty Dollar was periodically rebased to
keep its value in line with the precious metals, its value rose
substantially over time against the depreciating dollar. For
example, as already noted, a silver Liberty medallion with
a face value of $10 minted in 1998 contained one ounce
of 0.999 fine silver worth approximately $5 at the time of

6   Von NotHaus (2003) has a chapter devoted to the use of the Liberty
    Dollar as currency.

minting and sold then for $10. However, with silver valued at about $20 per ounce, this same medallion would have an intrinsic bullion value of about $20 and would typically trade for considerably more than this on eBay. Someone who bought such a medallion in 1998 would have had an investment that more than kept up with inflation, whereas someone who held onto a $10 banknote would have seen their investment lose about half its value over the period since 1998. Moreover, investors who bought gold Liberty Dollars rather than silver ones would have benefited considerably more.

The criticism could be made that, as a store of value, the Liberty Dollar was inferior to holding, say, pure silver as the latter would not have involved the minter's profit that led the Liberty Dollar to generally have a higher face value than its silver value. At the same time, it could be argued that, because the Liberty Dollar was not generally accepted, it was less useful than the Federal Reserve dollar as a means of exchange. In addition, because of the re-basing of the Liberty Dollars, prices would not be stable when expressed in the dollar unit of account. In response to these criticisms it should be noted that over the long run the Liberty Dollar would retain its value if the value of the dollar fell against precious metals because the Liberty Dollar would be revalued. At the same time, it had the potential to become generally acceptable and therefore be more useful than silver jewellery, trinkets, etc., as a medium of exchange. Indeed, as is noted above, it did become widely used in exchange even if it was not generally accepted.

The Liberty Dollar and the law in the land of liberty

The attitude of the government towards the Liberty Dollar was initially one of tolerance. However, the attitude then hardened. In 2006 the US Mint issued a press release stating that use of the Liberty Dollar was a federal crime.[7] In March 2007, von NotHaus filed a lawsuit against the Mint seeking a declaratory judgement that this allegation was untrue. The government responded with a raid by the FBI and the Secret Service on the Liberty Dollar offices in Evanston, Indiana, on 14 November 2007 in which they seized virtually everything they could, including gold and silver medallions, paper certificates, computers and even the furniture. The warehouse in Idaho where the gold and silver were kept for the Liberty Dollar paper and digital receipts was also raided. Approximately nine tons of gold and silver were seized, even though this was not even the property of the Liberty Dollar company, but that of its clients. This seizure made it impossible for the company to redeem the certificates.

A federal indictment was then brought against von NotHaus and three others in the United States District Court in Statesville, NC, in May 2009, and von NotHaus was arrested on 4 June. He was charged with counterfeiting,[8] fraud and conspiracy against the United States.

---

7   http://www.usmint.gov/pressroom/?action=press_release&id=710.

8   The word 'counterfeit' seems never to have been used, but the meaning is clear. To quote the US Attorney's Press Release of 18 March 2011, the charge was that the company had been 'making coins resembling and similar to United States coins' in violation of 18 USC § 485 quoted above.

The first charge can only be described as risible, for two reasons: firstly, counterfeiting requires some attempt to make the 'fake' currency look like the 'real' one, and yet the Liberty Dollar currency was quite different in appearance from official currency. The medallions themselves were easily distinguishable, even if they shared some similarities such as the dollar sign '$', the words 'dollar' and 'Liberty' and the year of minting. They differed in obvious ways: they included 'USA' (instead of 'United States of America') and 'Trust in God' (instead of 'In God We Trust'); they did not feature the Statue of Liberty or the phrase 'legal tender'; they also had other features not found on US coinage such as an image of Ron Paul, a toll free phone number and even a URL. They also differed from official US coinage in being made from precious metals instead of base metals. If these were ever meant to be counterfeit, they were certainly poor ones – and unnecessarily expensive to produce, being made of precious metal. The Liberty Dollar certificates were also very different from greenbacks. In fact, none were even green. They had the words 'Negotiable American Liberty Currency Silver [or where appropriate, Gold] Certificate' boldly emblazoned on one side and 'Warehouse Receipt' on the other, and so could hardly be mistaken for US currency. They also bear von NotHaus's own signature, whereas it is traditional for counterfeiters to keep their handiwork anonymous. They were even a different shape and size from greenbacks.

The second reason why the charge was risible is that any charge of counterfeiting implies fraud and intent to deceive, and yet there was never any evidence of any intent of fraud or misrepresentation.

If the Liberty Dollar is sufficiently similar to official currency to constitute a federal offence, then the government should pursue anyone who issues anything that could be construed as similar to the official currency. After all, there are many other private organisations that issue alternative dollar currencies even within the US. These include: issuers of travellers' cheques, such as American Express; Parker Brothers, who make the board game 'Monopoly'; and Disney Corporation, whose Disney Dollars are obvious counterfeits signed off by Scrooge McDuck.

Von NotHaus's defence was that he did not steal, defraud, misrepresent or force anyone to hold Liberty Dollars or do anything else illegal, and that his customers were satisfied, not least because the value of the Liberty Dollar had risen considerably over time while that of the US dollar depreciated.

This defence was, however, rejected and von NotHaus was convicted on 18 March 2011 of: making coins resembling and similar to United States coins; issuing, passing, selling, and possessing Liberty Dollar coins; uttering and passing unauthorised coins for use as current money; fraud; and conspiracy against the United States. He is currently free on an Appearance Bond, awaiting a potential sentence of up to 22 years in federal prison and a substantial fine.

The suspicion that von NotHaus was singled out because he was seen as subversive would appear to be borne out by a press release issued by the US Attorney's Office after the conviction. In this press release, US Attorney Anne Tompkins made a series of assertions so absurd that they have already become legendary. In particular, she asserted that: 'Attempts to undermine the legitimate currency of this country are simply a unique form of domestic terrorism.'

In response to this, it could be noted:

- There is nothing illegitimate about the Liberty Dollar, which was intended to improve US currency, both by providing a superior alternative to Federal Reserve currency and by providing an incentive for the Federal Reserve to improve its currency.
- The Liberty Dollar was succeeding until the government closed it down. Thus, the government is guilty of the very offence it condemns: that is, of undermining legitimate currency.
- Since the Federal Reserve took over responsibility for the currency in 1914, the purchasing power of the currency has fallen by over 95 per cent according to the government's consumer price index statistics. If this is not undermining the currency, one wonders what is.
- Since when is competing against a governmental organisation, such as the Federal Reserve, an act of terrorism? By the same logic, Federal Express must be guilty of terrorism because it competes with the US Post Office.
- To explain what should be obvious, 'terrorism' is defined by Webster's dictionary as 'the systematic use

of terror especially as a means of coercion'. Where is the 'terror' in the Liberty Dollar? In addition, the four US criminal codes that define terrorism stipulate violence as a required element. So how can we have terrorism without either violence or coercion?

The official press release by the US Department of Justice cited Article 1, Section 8, Clause 5 of the Constitution, which delegated to Congress the power to coin money and to regulate the value thereof. However, this same clause also indicates that the only constitutional money is coined money, and this can only be understood as gold and silver coinage: thus, inconvertible paper money is itself unconstitutional. Furthermore, the Constitution did not give Congress the authority to establish a money monopoly or a central bank, or indeed any bank at all. Consequently, the Federal Reserve and the money it issues are both unconstitutional. The government is therefore misrepresenting the Constitution by drawing selectively from it to suit itself. Legal expert Bill Rounds (2011) goes further and suggests that US Attorney Tompkins recklessly and negligently made false statements of the law regarding the Liberty Dollar case, violated ethics rules and defamed Mr von NotHaus in the process.

Ms Tompkins also made a second memorable assertion that makes as little sense as the first: 'While these forms of anti-government activities do not involve violence, they are every bit as insidious and represent a clear and present danger to the economic stability of this country.' Quite how the Liberty Dollar protecting the value of the currency that people use presents *any* danger to the country's economic stability she omitted to explain.

Leaving aside the absence of logic, the US Attorney's comments betray an elementary misunderstanding of the competitive process: in the provision of currency as with anything else, having a single monopoly provider leads to poor quality, and you only get good quality if you open the field up to competition. We saw this when the postal service was opened to competition. And it was *exactly* this public service that the Liberty Dollar was providing when it started to compete against the currency provided by the Federal Reserve, which by any reasonable standard is certainly of low quality, because it is depreciating all the time – while the Liberty Dollar was appreciating in value. The root fallacy here is the old idea that 'money' is something best provided by an inefficient government monopoly that needs to be protected from competition.[9]

---

9   There is a very interesting historical parallel of the type of mind-shift required to be able to understand the basic issues. Before Ronald Coase, it was taken as self-evident that radio broadcasting wavelengths should be allocated by government bureaucrats. Coase then came up with the idea that broadcasting wavelengths could be allocated by auction only to be met with incredulity and resistance. When he presented his views in testimony to a Federal Communications Commission hearing on the future of broadcasting, a Commissioner rebuked him for making a joke at the expense of the hearing! Invited to prepare a report on the subject for the Rand Corporation, Coase and his colleagues met with the most severe criticism and Rand refused to publish the report in the unshakeable conviction that the broadcasting spectrum was by definition a public good.

The guilty verdict was greeted with widespread disbelief. One blogger commented that it must be 'a funny kind of counterfeiting operation' when a one-ounce silver coin marked $20 was now worth $38.50 on silver content alone. Another remarked sadly, 'If we are not free to voluntarily exchange goods and services for gold and silver, then indeed US currency is backed by bullets.' A recurring theme in the blogosphere reaction was that von NotHaus was being persecuted for performing a public service. To quote from one such reaction:[10]

Say Hello to Domestic Terrorist Bernard von NotHaus.

Bernard ... is the architect of the Liberty Dollar [which] is in no way meant to be legal tender ... looks nothing like real U.S. minted coins and you would have to be blind to think they looked the least bit similar ... He did not harm anyone. He defrauded no one. In fact, thousands of people are now wealthier and richer, because of him.

Here is the irony. Well, it is more like a travesty. On the one hand you have the federal government and its bureaucrats attempting to punish a good and decent man and at the same time try to reverse thousands of years of TRADITION of Gold and Silver being money, as it is implied in the constitution. And on the other hand, you have the Liberty Dollar, which is worth far more today than it was in 2007 before the federal government raided and confiscated them. So if you did in fact trade your worthless federal notes for actual Silver and Gold like Bernard von NotHaus intended you to, you would be much more wealthy today because the value of that metal has skyrocketed.

---

10 The irony of Bernard Von NotHaus, www.silvermovement.com, 2 February 2012 (website now offline).

As for the Liberty Dollar, the company actually had its best year in 2008, after the FBI raid, but the company was forced to cease operations after von NotHaus was arrested in 2009.

However, new mints are opening up and appear to be doing good business based on the Liberty Dollar model that von NotHaus pioneered. These include the Aspen Dollar, the New Liberty Dollar, which is similar to the old Liberty Dollar but has some extra stay-out-of-jail features[11] and the Second Amendment Dollar that is issued out of Bud's Gun Shop at 1105 Industry Rd, Lexington, KY. As Bud's site explains, 'BudsGunShop.com, a proud supporter of the Second Amendment, is pleased to offer our Second Amendment Dollar with volume pricing so everyone can commemorate his and her right to Protect Life ... *NOTICE: Second Amendment Dollar is not intended to be used as United States currency and any representation as such is strictly prohibited by law.*'

---

11 http://www.newlibertydollar.com. The design of the New Liberty Dollar was based on a forensic analysis of what went wrong for the defence at the von NotHaus trial and therefore addresses the more obvious legal vulnerabilities faced by private minters that came up in that case. For example, the New Liberty Dollar omits any appearance of 'USA', 'TRUST IN GOD' is replaced by 'RIGHT TO CONTRACT' and buyers are asked to affirm that they understand that they are not getting government coin that relies on legal tender for its value, but are instead getting a product that derives its value from its precious metal content, its numismatic appeal and so on. It will be interesting to see how the legal geniuses at the DOJ handle this one.

Returning to von NotHaus, he is still awaiting senten-cing and the case has become a *cause célèbre* not just in the US but worldwide.[12] A motion for acquittal or retrial was filed in March 2013 and is a model of eloquence:

> Mr. von NotHaus stands convicted of various statutorily-defined forms of counterfeiting. The irony of this is that if anything is clear from the evidence presented at trial, it is that the last thing Mr. von NotHaus wanted was for Liberty Dollars to be confused with coins issued by the United States government. That would, as witness Ver-non Robinson testified, have defeated the whole purpose – to demonstrate to citizens and communities that there is a way to engage in commerce and not use the Federal Reserve system.
>
> Whether writing scholarly papers on value-based cur-rency, attracting media attention, or selling T-shirts say-ing 'The Fed Can Bite Me,' Mr. von NotHaus has always operated out in the open. His intention – to protest the Federal Reserve system – has always been plain. The jury's verdict conflates a program created to function

---

12 There was also a second trial, in which holders of the silver and gold seized by the government in the Idaho raid sought to have their property returned. In a memorable judgement, Judge Martin Reidinger denounced the government in no uncertain terms. He said: (1) 'the Government have completely lost sight of the purpose of this proceeding and the purpose of the forfeiture statute.' (2) 'The Government seeks to deprive them [the petitioners] of their hard-earned retirement funds and assets based on absurd contortions of the forfeiture statute.' (3) 'This is the sort of behaviour that di-minishes the public trust in government, as well as the justice sys-tem in general.' The ruling is available at http://www.libertydollar news.org/2013june/2013_02_25_reidinger_dismisal_order.pdf.

as an alternative to the Federal Reserve system with one designed to deceive people into believing it was the very thing Mr. von NotHaus was protesting in the first place.

Whatever one's opinion about the merit of value-based currency, the fact remains that the Liberty Dollar was not a counterfeit and was not intended to function as such. The verdict is a perversion of the counterfeiting statutes and should be set aside.[13]

---

13 The motion for acquittal is available on the web at http://www.gata. org/files/VonNotHausRetrialMotion-03-25-2013.pdf.

3   DIGITAL CURRENCY

Digital currency takes many different forms and there are thousands of different schemes. What they all have in common is electronic stored value systems – networks of exchange and value accounts that store financial value to be used to pay for goods and services. The most conventional are debit card, credit card and comparable systems (for example, PayPal) that allow payments in the existing official unit of account. However, many others use their own unit of account. These include those operated by many large corporations that run loyalty reward systems denominated in 'points' or 'miles' – one thinks of the frequent flyer systems operated by airlines, innumerable grocery store reward systems and so on – many of which are morphing into digital monetary systems.

Examples of digital currency also include many internet-based currency systems that have come and gone over the years. High profile casualties included Flooz and Beenz, which were casualties of the dotcom crash (and, in the former case, of Whoopi Goldberg's advertising as well); these blossomed briefly, but never really caught on and both firms failed in August 2001. More recent examples are Facebook Credits, which allow users to purchase virtual goods on Facebook applications, and Microsoft Points, which is the digital currency used by the Xbox Live Marketplace and the Zune store. Both, however, are now being phased out by their sponsoring organisations. Two other well-publicised recent examples of digital currency are Ven[1] and Liberty Reserve.[2] These examples also illustrate how diverse digital currencies can be.

Digital gold currency

An important class of digital currencies is digital gold currency (DGC): digital payment systems in which the unit of

---

1 Ven grew out of a Facebook application launched in July 2007 and was launched on the general web in January 2011 as what its authors enthusiastically describe as 'an open payment digital ecosystem'. Ven is a digital currency traded among members of the Hub Culture network system and is targeted at people who want to have their own currency system and save the rainforests at the same time. Hard verifiable facts about the size of the Ven monetary system and how it actually operates are difficult to come by, but one gets the impression that Ven is still a fairly small-scale digital currency.

2 Liberty Reserve was a Costa Rica–based digital currency company that was shut down by US federal prosecutors in May 2013. Prosecutors alleged that criminal activity went largely undetected because the company made no effort to verify the identities of its users, which made it attractive for scam artists and money launderers. The founder Arthur Budovsky and six others were themselves charged with money laundering as well as with operating an unlicensed money-transfer company. Liberty Reserve was said to have been used to launder more than $6 billion in criminal proceeds and to have had one million clients when it was closed down.

account is gold and in which user accounts are backed by gold reserves. Examples include e-gold, e-Bullion, Gold-Money and Pecunix. A user would buy DGC units using conventional payments methods (such as a wire transfer) and transfer units to another account holder, who could then cash out his holding. Such systems provide an attractive way to effect international payments transactions, as they make such transactions inexpensive and, at least in the early days, to some extent anonymous. Initially, they were also beyond the reach of bank regulations (as providers are not banks) and regulations governing money transfer (as the transfers were not of legal money per se but of claims to units of gold). Since they emerged, however, governments have fought hard – with success – to bring them under their control.

One feature of these systems is that of irreversibility: reversing transactions is difficult if not impossible even in the case of error, unauthorised use or the failure of a vendor to provide goods. This feature makes DGC transactions akin to cash transactions. Irreversibility makes for lower operating costs, instant clearing and ready access to transferred 'funds'. In this they differ from many conventional systems (such as credit or debit card systems) that allow customers to dispute or reverse transfers, but which are more costly and typically slower.

e-gold

Perhaps the best-known DGC system is e-gold, a company founded in 1996 by Doug Jackson, a libertarian oncologist with a passion for Austrian economics.[3] e-gold was envisaged as a private international gold currency. It was based in Melbourne, FL, but registered in Nevis in the Caribbean: Dr Jackson argued that it was not covered by existing US financial regulation not just because of its 'offshore' status, but also because it was a payment system rather than a *money* transmitter or bank. Legally, he was correct: US laws and regulations relating to financial institutions relied upon definitions of 'currency' and 'funds' that excluded e-gold.

e-gold was very user-friendly. Accounts could be set up in minutes, and initially there was no checking of names or identity and little monitoring of customer accounts. Customers could purchase units of e-gold using a credit card or a wire transfer, e-gold units were easily and quickly transferred to other e-gold account holders, and cashing out was straightforward. Fees were very low.

By 2005, e-gold had grown to become second only to PayPal in the online payments industry: it had 1.2 million accounts and transactions that year totalled $1.5 billion. It had become a worldwide enterprise, ideal for international transactions. At its peak, the currency was backed by 3.8 tonnes of physical gold held in London and Dubai valued at more than $85m, greater than the official gold reserves of Canada.

---

3 Though we should not forget, of course, that the Liberty Dollar – or rather its digital version – was another form of DCG. Some background on e-gold can be found in Grow et al. (2006) and Zetter (2009). Also recommended is White (forthcoming).

One also has to bear in mind that it operated over a period where there was considerable regulatory uncertainty. Jackson's argument was there was no intent to avoid regulation as such but, rather, there was no applicable regulation and hence no sense of anything to avoid. The choice of Nevis was motivated by other considerations. The first was that strong encryption was being treated by the government at the time as if it were a munition, raising tricky issues of export and international use: this made it difficult for a US-based entity to offer services that might involve encryption to foreigners. A second was that the company wanted a base with a strong track record for observing the primacy and sanctity of contract – and the US could not provide this in light of its poor record of gold expropriation.

The popularity of e-gold came with a downside, however: it became very popular with online criminals too, who saw it as an anonymous way of moving money around.[4] Far from turning a blind eye, as he was later accused of doing, Jackson did investigate suspicious clients and turned over the results of his investigations to law enforcement agencies. As he wrote to me:

---

4 It was widely said that transactions on e-gold were anonymous, but in private correspondence Dr Jackson is emphatic that e-gold never promoted itself as anonymous and explicitly dispelled any such impression. The government's argument that e-gold was providing anonymity was also rejected by the judge at the subsequent trial. Jackson informs me that it was US law enforcement itself that started to disseminate this claim around 2001.

practically speaking, e-gold was the opposite of anonymous. We could and did connect the dots that enable identification of the most disciplined of chameleons. Even Russian virtuosos, with impeccable anonymizing techniques were at the mercy of transactional counterparties who might be dumb wannabe punks living in Omaha in their grandma's basement. A Spend to or from an idiot would create a permanent link flagging them in our database.

e-gold investigators were instrumental in identifying and locating the crème de la crème of international hard case cyber criminals, a cohort whose career-ending mistake was to believe the misinformation about e-gold being anonymous...

Apart from anything else, the idea that e-gold was anonymous made no business sense. The company's experience was that most people valued convenience over anonymity. To quote Jackson again:

> The reality was the person who thought they were being clever by signing up as Mickey Mouse was risking loss of their Account; if they lost their passphrase, as even clever people do from time to time, and their point of contact information was worthless, they were left with no way to validate their bonafides and have their account access restored by e-gold Customer Service. The Account Agreement required people to provide correct identifiers and no one was exposed to greater risk than tricky people who did not comply.

> Moreover, while still on this misunderstood topic of anonymity, the genuine bad guy trying to operate anonymously using e-gold was almost certain to be tracked down. This was due to the combination of a closed system that kept *everything*, plus e-gold's international network

of correspondents ... since all too often they were the victims of exploits such as (conventional) payment repudiation due to fraud. This global network was comprised of the independent providers of exchange services, each with their own database containing a wealth of additional identifiers as well as session information (IPs, timestamps, sometimes (browser) agent-tags) and data regarding accounts and usage in/of external payment systems.

Over time, the pressure from law enforcement agencies increased. It was no longer enough merely to comply with legal subpoenas but e-gold was increasingly expected to proactively monitor its clients and report its results. The company complied too.

The criminals discovered included the mob, drug dealers and con artists peddling Ponzi schemes and credit card scams. They also included an outfit called Shadow Crew, an international cybercrime syndicate with 4,000 members worldwide, which was engaged in massive identity theft and fraud and used e-gold as a vehicle to launder the proceeds of its crimes. One of its members, Omar Dhanani, boasted on a chat room in 2004 that he moved between $40,000 and $100,000 a week through e-gold. Another case involved a criminal who went by the pseudonym 'segvec' and who was engaged in the biggest credit card scam of all time: he was not even on law enforcement's radar until Jackson discovered his suspicious activities; they then got involved after he informed them and persuaded themselves that he was Ukrainian. Meanwhile, Jackson tracked him down to Florida and he turned out to be Albert Gonzalez, a criminal informant working at the time for the Secret Service, operating out of their offices, on their stipend.

The law enforcement services then turned on e-gold: its premises were raided by the Secret Service on 16 December 2005 and its principals indicted in April 2007. The charges boiled down to e-gold being an unlicensed money transmitting entity and a de facto means of moving the proceeds of illegal activities; it was also alleged that the principals had tacit knowledge of this activity but had done nothing about it.[5] The charges were never proven, but facing a possible 20 years in jail and a $500,000 fine, in July 2008 Jackson agreed to a plea bargain and in November was sentenced to six months of home detention, three years' supervision, 300 hours' community service and a small fine. As Jackson explained afterwards in an email:

> Our case was lost when the judge made a ruling in response to our motion to dismiss that was so prejudicial that, in conjunction with what we were then told regarding the horrifying perversion of the doctrine of 'relevant conduct' [used in federal sentencing guidelines[6]], would

5   The allegation that e-gold had done nothing to combat criminals using their system is demonstrably false and conceded by the government itself. The reason for law enforcement agencies turning on e-gold is, however, unclear. From the perspective of US law enforcement as a whole, given the quality catches that e-gold had been bringing in, taking the firm down can only be regarded as a spectacular own goal.

6   Dr Jackson was right to be worried. As Chetson (2011) explains, the concept of relevant conduct 'allows the judge to punish the defendant for uncharged crimes, or crimes for which a jury acquitted

have made it insanely reckless to risk an even worse miscarriage.

Even the judge acknowledged that Jackson had not committed any fraud or intended to break the law, and confirmed the veracity of the company's audited gold reserve; she also departed from federal sentencing guidelines to hand down a much smaller sentence that acknowledged that Dr Jackson had been operating in good faith. e-gold was thereafter wound down.

And so another worthwhile American private money experiment ended in a miscarriage of justice. The key question was whether e-gold was a money transmitter: e-gold took the view it was not because it did not transmit cash and the statutes themselves were ambiguous. One should keep in mind the official line that gold is no longer money. However, the court ruled against and it was this ruling that pushed the company into the July 2008 plea agreement. Yet, at the same time, the government itself admitted that the law was unclear:

(found not guilty!) the defendant, when sentencing the defendant following the conviction on even tenuously related charges.' The implications are disturbing, to say the least. For instance, if a defendant goes to trial and is acquitted by a jury of his peers of trafficking, he may be punished for trafficking by the judge if he's convicted of any tangentially related charge by the jury. The system is so absurd – it fundamentally turns the putative Constitutional 5th, 6th, 8th and 14th Amendments on their heads – that it creates a system where about 98 per cent of all defendants plead guilty as part of agreements out of fear that even if they were to win everything (except a minor related charge), they would be sentenced by the judge in spite of those acquittals (Chetson 2011).

Digital currencies are on the forefront of international fund transfers. e-gold is the most prominent digital currency out there. It has the attention of the entire digital currency world. That world is a bit of a wild west right now. *People are looking for what are the rules* and what are the consequences.

Laurel L. Rimon, Dept of Justice Sentencing Transcript,
p. 95.2, my emphasis.

As further testament as to the ambiguity of the statutes, Broox W. Peterson, Sarah Jane Hughes and Stephen T. Middlebrook, a Senior Counsel at the US Department of the Treasury and co-chair of the Working Group on Electronic Payments Systems, published an article in November 2007 – after the e-gold indictment and before the plea agreement – which indicated, specifically related to the e-gold case, that the four federal statutes relevant to money transmitting:

all contain different definitions of 'money transmitter' ... Because e-gold is operating outside the traditional realm of money transmitters, it is necessary to explore the nuances of the statutory definitions in order to determine *whether* the laws encompass e-gold. The inconsistencies in the statutes, coupled with potential criminal penalties in § 1960(a), 185 make advising clients who want to implement novel new payment mechanisms a difficult task. [My emphasis.]

There was also a big regulatory clean-up afterwards to make sure that digital gold companies were properly regulated – an effort that would not have been necessary if the government case against e-gold had been a solid one in the first place.

Before the December 2005 raid, the company had never been contacted by any governmental agency to inform it that it was acting illegally. In fact, it was *already* in discussions with the IRS to establish its regulatory status. The government examiners had informed e-gold that they would make a determination and the raid occurred before they responded.

There were also serious doubts about the legality of the Secret Service raid itself. In an emergency hearing thirteen days after the raid, Judge John M. Facciola complained that he had been misled by the government when he had been asked to sign the initial search and seizure warrants. As he put it to the government's lawyers:

> In the ordinary course I would review [a seizure warrant in a criminal case] on the spot and sign it or not sign it. But in the [e-gold] seizure, I immediately recognized my concern...
>
> What you have here are allegations being flung ... without an evidentiary basis on which to rule. Now by virtue of you going the way you did [ex parte allegations of child pornography to obtain a seizure warrant in a civil licensing case: that is, government lies to get the judge to sign the warrants KD] you circumvented the Federal Rules of Civil Procedure...
>
> It never occurred to me in my wildest dreams ... that far from operating surreptitiously, there have been negotiations with this company and the Internal Revenue Service as to the precise issue you raise about transmitting

money and being subject to that statute, the Bank Secrecy Act.

Unfortunately, the company was denied an evidentiary hearing showing probable cause despite an appeals court ruling that the law entitles defendants to an opportunity to be heard where access to assets is necessary for the exercise of the Sixth Amendment right to counsel.[7]

The lessons to be learned are fairly clear. To paraphrase Jackson, if you run any business in this area:

- You are responsible for compliance, with or without regulatory clarity. Forget about reasonable doubt or goodwill for helping catch criminals and fraudsters.
- If you move or facilitate movement of funds, you are most likely a money transmitter whether you know that or not.
- If your intent is honest and you are honest, you can still fall foul of the law.
- The government may act quickly, aggressively and without warning.
- Get a good lawyer ... the government might just want to 'send a message' at your expense.

7　There were also other repercussions that were overlooked or ignored by the government. It wasn't until 2013 that an agreement was reached to allow e-gold's customers to redeem their holdings, so their wealth was tied up by the government for nearly eight years. As for e-gold, the plea agreement itself involved a farcical aspect: it called for the company to become compliant with relevant legislation, but nobody involved noticed that by accepting the plea agreement the principals would become felons and therefore automatically ineligible to obtain banking licenses.

If one compares this case with the Liberty Dollar, one immediately notices worrying parallels: two decent businessmen operating out in the open, operating under the rule of law but trying to offer alternative monetary systems in one form or another, and both taken down by government agencies that were arguably operating outside the law themselves and have never been held to account – in essence, the victims of arbitrary government attack.[8]

---

8 Another DGC company is GoldMoney, founded in 2001 and run by James Turk from Jersey in the Channel Islands. This provided both gold bailment and DGC services. This firm was widely regarded as the market leader in the gold currency sector and had over $2bn of assets in storage by 2011. However, in January 2012 it withdrew from the DGC business citing the impact of new regulations that made the business unprofitable. GoldMoney was, therefore, yet another casualty of the government – in this case the UK government.

4   CRYPTOCURRENCY: BITCOIN

A more radical, indeed revolutionary, private currency is Bitcoin[1] – the most successful, though not the first,[2] of a new type of currency known as cryptocurrency. This is a form of highly anonymous computer currency based on the use of cryptography to control the creation and transfer of money. The designers of cryptocurrency sought to create not just a new currency, but a new anarchist social order. To quote one of the pioneers in this area, Wei Dai, in 1998, the objective is to achieve a crypto-anarchy[3] in which:

---

1   For more information about Bitcoin – in addition to the sources cited in this article – a good source is Jon Matonis's blog, The Monetary Future (http://themonetaryfuture.blogspot.co.uk/). Lew Rockwell also has some good commentary on Bitcoin on his site, LewRockwell.com.

2   The first cryptocurrency was B-money. This was invented by Wei Dai in 1998 and was a direct precursor to Bitcoin but did not catch on due to its impracticality. In particular, it required that all transactions be broadcast to all participants, each of whom was to keep a record of them; it also stipulated a rather cumbersome dispute resolution procedure.

3   The notion of crypto-anarchy was first put forward by Tim May in his 'Crypto-Anarchist Manifesto' announced to like-minded techno-anarchists at 'Crypto 88'. The most distinctive feature of

the government is not temporarily destroyed but permanently forbidden and permanently unnecessary. It's a community where the threat of violence is impotent because violence is impossible, and violence is impossible because its participants cannot be linked to their true names or physical locations.[4]

Bitcoin was invented in 2009 by an anonymous programmer using the *nom de plume* Satoshi Nakamoto.[5] Its key innovation, relative to earlier forms of digital currency, is that it is completely decentralised and has no central authority or organiser whatever.

Bitcoin is a type of e-cash system in which there is no central body to authorise or track transactions; instead, these tasks are carried out collectively by the network itself. Transactions are carried out using a digital 'coin' that uses public-key cryptography. When a coin is transferred from *A* to *B*, *A* adds *B*'s public key to the coin and digitally signs the coin using a private key. *B* then owns the coin and can transfer it further. The network collectively maintains a public list of all previous transactions and before any coin is processed, it is checked by the network to ensure

---

crypto-anarchism is the use of cryptography to protect the privacy of consensual economic arrangements from state interference, and so evade both censorship and prohibition.

4   http://www.weidai.com/bmoney.txt

5   The identity of Satoshi Nakamoto has spawned a media mystery hunt reminiscent of, but already much bigger than, the searches for Shergar and Lord Lucan, and with equal success. Despite many claims to the contrary, his/her/their true identity remains unknown.

that the user hasn't already spent it. This prevents a user from illicitly spending the same coin over and over again.

Nakamoto himself gave a clear explanation of the thinking behind Bitcoin in an email announcing its launch on 11 February 2009:

> The root problem with conventional currency is all the trust that is required to make it work. The central bank must be trusted not to debase the currency, but the history of fiat currencies is full of breaches of that trust...
>
> A generation ago, multi-user time-sharing computer systems had a similar problem. Before strong encryption, users had to rely on password protection to secure their files, placing trust in the system administrator to keep their information private. Privacy could always be overridden by the admin based on his judgment call weighing the principle of privacy against other concerns, or at the request of his superiors. Then strong encryption became available to the masses, and trust was no longer required. Data could be secured in a way that was physically impossible to access, no matter for what reason, no matter how good the excuse, no matter what.
>
> It's time we had the same thing for money. With e-currency based on cryptographic proof, without the need to trust a third party middleman, money can be secure and transactions complete.
>
> One of the fundamental building blocks for such a system is digital signatures. A digital coin contains the public key of its owner. To transfer it, the owner signs the coin together with the public key of the next owner. Anyone can check the signatures to verify the chain of ownership. [This] works well to secure ownership, but leaves one big problem unsolved: double-spending. Any owner could try to re-spend an already spent coin by signing it again

to another owner. The usual solution is for a trusted company with a central database to check for double-spending, but that just gets back to the trust model...

Bitcoin's solution is to use a peer-to-peer network to check for double-spending ... the result is a distributed system with no single point of failure.[6]

The supply of Bitcoin

Bitcoins are created in a process known as 'mining'. This process uses up computer power to search for solutions to pseudo-random number computational problems in a way analogous to a gold miner looking for gold. Finding solutions is not easy, but when a Bitcoin 'miner' hits upon a solution, he is rewarded with Bitcoin that he can spend. The solution is then verified by the network: unlike finding a solution, verifying one is easy. The process is designed in a way that ensures that the amounts produced are almost exactly known in advance. Anyone can mine for Bitcoin, but the network adjusts the difficulty of 'finding' Bitcoin to the number of active 'miners' and the computer power used in a way that was initially set to generate a production rate of 50 Bitcoin every ten minutes. This initial rate halved in late November 2012 and will keeping halving thereafter every four years, and the rules are constructed so that the total amount 'mined' can never exceed 21 million.

The projected supply of Bitcoin is therefore highly predictable and is shown by the black line in Figure 1: the supply rises at a periodically decreasing rate to approach

---

6   http://p2pfoundation.ning.com/forum/topics/bitcoin-open-source

Figure 1 **Stock of Bitcoin**

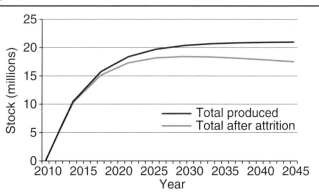

a limiting value of 21 million as production of new Bitcoin gradually fizzles out. However, as with other forms of currency, when considering supply we also have to take account of attrition – Bitcoin disappearing because people lose data wallets containing their Bitcoin codes, lose their encryption codes or experience hard drive failures with no backup. Accordingly, the grey line gives the projected supply of Bitcoin assuming an illustrative attrition rate of 0.5 per cent per year. In this case, we see that the projected stock of Bitcoin taking account of attrition rises to a peak of about 18.4 million in 2029 and thereafter falls.

As a consequence, leaving aside the possibility of some internal flaw or disaster that destroys the system, the only real uncertainty about the future supply of Bitcoin relates to the attrition rate.[7]

---

7   Bitcoin is often compared with gold and it is true that both have highly inelastic supply schedules in the short run. However, they

The demand for Bitcoin

Turning to the demand side, the first question is why any-one would demand Bitcoin, that is, be willing to trade any-thing of value for it. One argument is that people would demand Bitcoin for use as a medium of exchange *if* they believe that other people would accept it in payments, but then why would they believe that? The traditional answer in monetary theory is that starting *de novo*, people would be prepared to accept X – whether X be paper, Bitcoin, gold or anything else – as possible money *only if* it had some al-ternative non-monetary use. If it has no alternative use – if it is intrinsically useless – then there is a first mover prob-lem: no one would be the first to trade for X, and X would never get off the ground as money. Consequently, although it is *possible* to conceive of an equilibrium in which each accepts X as money because others do so, we would never get there because X would never get started as money: the potential new currency X would be permanently stuck on its launch pad. The implication is that Bitcoin could never get started as a new currency.

Yet, however it managed to do so, the plain fact is that Bitcoin has already taken off as a currency, so arguing

---

differ in that Bitcoin has a very inelastic supply schedule in the long run as well, whereas the long-run supply of gold is more elastic. They also differ in that the long-run supply of Bitcoin is perfectly predictable (if one ignores attrition), but the future stock of gold is less predictable because of the possibility of unexpected gold dis-coveries or improvements to extraction technology.

that it could not is akin to haggling over the possibility of human flight after just watching the Wright brothers.[8]

A possible explanation for its successful takeoff might simply be that early trades were among a small group of enthusiasts who shared a similar mindset and commitment to the Bitcoin enterprise;[9] they managed to get it up and running on a small scale[10] and other people gradually joined it as it became clear that the Bitcoin system was working – and especially when it became apparent that

---

8 Thus, regardless of monetary economists' theoretical arguments over whether it should exist or not, the demand for Bitcoin already exists – and the fact that monetary economists might not understand it is another matter.

9 An analogy here is with the early adoption of Esperanto as a new language: the exact same argument (that is, that no one would move first) would similarly 'prove' that Esperanto couldn't take off either. Yet it did, up to a point.

10 This explanation fits with what is known about the genesis of the Bitcoin market. The earliest Bitcoiners shared a communitarian spirit. Shortly after Bitcoin started, Gavin Andresen bought 10,000 Bitcoin for $50 and then gave them away to encourage their use. The first 'real' trade then took place when Lazslo Hanyecx paid 10,000 Bitcoin for a pizza delivery (an expensive pizza even then; this involved paying a volunteer to order a transatlantic credit card delivery from England). In one of his last public statements in December 2010, in response to a suggestion that Bitcoin be accepted by Wikileaks, Nakamoto weighed in strongly against on the grounds that the Bitcoin project was not ready and still vulnerable (Wallace 2011): 'No, don't bring it on,' he wrote. 'The project needs to grow gradually so the software can be strengthened along the way. To Wikileaks I make this appeal not to try to use bitcoin. Bitcoin is a small beta community in its infancy. You would not stand to get more than pocket change, and the heat you would bring would likely destroy us at this stage.'

the anonymity of Bitcoin made it ideally suited for illegal trades.

This suggests that a key factor driving the demand for Bitcoin is the transactions demand for contraband purposes. The anonymity of Bitcoin also suggests a demand for Bitcoin for tax evasion, escaping capital controls, money laundering and similar purposes, and a store of value demand in which people use Bitcoin to escape financial repression by their own governments. However, we should not overlook the potential of Bitcoin for mundane legal transactions as well. After all, transactions are straightforward, inexpensive, fast and irreversible; they are also highly secure and potentially untraceable.

History of the Bitcoin market

It is interesting to examine how Bitcoin market prices and the quantities traded have behaved to date.[11] The former are shown in Figure 2.[12] The first trade occurred on 25 April 2010 and the first Bitcoin price was three cents. Early prices and quantities were low and it was almost three months before the first end-of-day price reached ten cents. However, once it got going, the market price rose strongly, peaked at nearly $30 in June 2011 and fell back sharply; it then gradually recovered and in March and (especially)

---

11 A very informative history of the early days of Bitcoin can be found in Wallace (2011).

12 These data refer to end-of-day prices starting from 13 September 2011.

Figure 2 **Bitcoin market prices ($)**

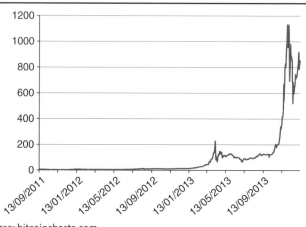

Source: bitcoincharts.com.

April 2013 rose strongly again to peak at almost $215 on 8 April; it then fell back to just over $63 eight days later, rallied again and shot up to around $1,200 in late November and early December, before falling back again to its latest (as of 10 January 2014) value of $923.70. These highlights mask a considerable amount of day-to-day and intraday volatility as well. In short, the price has risen enormously[13] since the market started but also been very volatile, and the market survived several major crashes that some thought would have destroyed it.

---

13 The rise in price from three cents to over $900 occurred in about three and a half years. Given such a return, it is safe to speculate that the demand for Bitcoin might include a considerable speculative component.

Since the supply of Bitcoin has been stable, this price volatility can only be ascribed to a volatile demand. It can be partly explained by occasional attacks and associated attempts at market manipulation, and by occasional bursts of publicity. An example of the former occurred in June 2011 when a hacker got into the Mt. Gox website and stimulated a massive sell-off, after which the price of Bitcoin plummeted. Examples of the latter were the very rapid surges in Bitcoin prices that followed highly publicised articles on Bitcoin in *Forbes* on 20 April 2011 and in *Gawker* on 1 June 2011, which served to introduce the currency to new users. Prices on the exchange also fell frequently in response to bad publicity, which was a common occurrence too.

Current state of the Bitcoin market

Bitcoin has regularly been in the news and it is possible that this section will be overtaken by events relatively quickly. The information in this section was last updated in January 2014.

Once Bitcoin took off, it soon became apparent that a major source of demand came from those trading on an anonymous exchange called Silk Road that was founded in February 2011 and specialised in trading illegal drugs. The size of this market is hard to determine and estimates of its size and rate of growth vary widely: estimates on the Silk Road forum in mid 2012 put the number of customers between 30,000 and 150,000. However, a study of Silk Road by Crispin (2012) suggested that the size of the market was smaller than this range. Studying the market over eight months to mid 2012, he estimated that the market had a total revenue of about $1.9 million per month by this point, with the numbers of sellers increasing. It generated a monthly commission to the exchange of about $143,000. He also identified a tight coupling between Silk Road and the Mt. Gox exchange, and estimated that daily sales on Silk Road corresponded to about 20 per cent of the Mt. Gox activity. More recently, Crispin has been quoted as saying that the volume of trading on Silk Road nearly doubled over the period over which he studied it (Franklin 2013), and by March 2013 was already far bigger than it was when his fieldwork ended (Ball 2013).

Bitcoin is being used for ordinary legal transactions as well. Bitcoin is already widely used in the Kreuzberg area of Berlin, for instance, but is also accepted in payment across the world and is rapidly growing in popularity. Reasons cited for using Bitcoin included it having lower transactions costs and being cheaper for retailers than credit cards: such reasons suggest the potential for considerable future growth in the 'legitimate' use of Bitcoin.[14] There were also reports of Bitcoin ATMs, which would exchange dollars for

---

14 Bitcoin is also extensively used for online trading. It is accepted and traded on or by a large number of exchanges and financial institutions, and is widely accepted on sites specialising in gambling, gaming, entertainment, music, marketing and web services; a large but partial list of sites accepting Bitcoin can be found at https://en.bitcoin.it/wiki/Trade. Well-known organisations accepting Bitcoin include Reddit, the Internet Archive, WordPress, Mega, Virgin and Wikileaks.

Bitcoin, and of companies starting to pay their employees in Bitcoin: for example, in March 2013, Expensify started to offer to pay its non-US employees in Bitcoin to avoid the high charges of PayPal.

There are also various forms of *physical* Bitcoin – in essence physical tokens convertible into real (that is, electronic) Bitcoin, which can be used in hand-to-hand exchange. These include physical Bitcoin coins (known as Casascius Bitcoin) and Bitbills (plastic cards or 'Bitcoin notes'). Both these have hologram-protected sealed components containing the keys to access a Bitcoin. These can circulate as hand-to-hand currency, their value assured by their convertibility into digital Bitcoin. At any time, the seal can be broken and the key recovered to allow the digital Bitcoin to be spent, but once the seal is broken it becomes obvious that the coin has been spent; it is then essentially worthless. Similar digital-to-physical Bitcoin innovations include PrintCoin, which is similar to cheques or debit cards drawn on Bitcoin accounts, and Firmcoin, which is essentially a reloadable Bitbill. Thus, a mere two years after its beginning, Bitcoin achieved the remarkable distinction of being the first currency in history to go from digital to physical rather than the other way round.[15]

---

15 One also sees the emergence of Bitcoin financial derivatives: these currently consist of futures, options and Contracts for Difference. New accounts are also being offered by brokers and exchanges to allow short selling and margin trading in Bitcoin, and Bitcoin hedge funds and Exchange Traded Funds are starting to appear. These should facilitate both risk management and speculation in Bitcoin markets and also deepen and increase liquidity in those markets.

Threats to Bitcoin

Bitcoin is, however, vulnerable to threats. One source of threats is cryptographic. Modern cryptographic systems depend on the assumption that an attacker would need a very long time – decades in fact – to decrypt a message, and it has been argued that this could change in the face of future advances in technology (for example, the development of quantum computers) or in mathematics (for example, new algorithms). Major advances in computing technology are surely inevitable, but Bitcoin automatically corrects for improvements in cryptographic technology or computational power by increasing the difficulty parameter[16] in the Bitcoin mining technology. Routine (or even not so routine) improvements in computational power should therefore pose no problem.

However, the possibility of a development that completely breaks the cryptography cannot be ruled out: it is not as if 'undecipherable' codes haven't been broken before. The nightmare scenario, in this context, is where a virus or a huge leap in raw computer power leads the public key feature of Bitcoin to be broken open to reveal the identities behind all the Bitcoin trades that have ever taken place.

Another threat is from botnets – large networks of home PCs that are taken over by a virus and then controlled

---

16 This parameter controls the overall rate of Bitcoin production. It is calculated approximately every 14 days, and then reset to keep the overall mining rate of the whole network at an approximately constant rate, now set to one block every 20 minutes.

remotely.[17] These 'zombie armies' can then be used for various nefarious purposes but two in particular are relevant to Bitcoin.[18]

The first is to mount distributed denial-of-service (DDoS) attacks against Bitcoin exchanges. Essentially, the target site is overwhelmed with too much traffic in an attempt to disrupt its activities. This has happened on a number of occasions, and the most notable target is Mt. Gox. The motives for such attacks would appear to be to destabilise Bitcoin by undermining confidence in the exchange,

---

17 Another threat is from Internet theft, but there is nothing in this problem unique to Bitcoin, and the lesson is not to cut corners on security. Individual users of Bitcoin can protect themselves using 'off-line wallets' that remain secure even if their computers are infected. They can also protect their Bitcoin wallets by trying not to lose them: one early Bitcoiner was reported to have had three copies of his wallet, but inadvertently managed to erase two of them and then lost his password for the third, in the process losing $140,000 worth of Bitcoin. They should also not skimp on common sense when it comes to storing their Bitcoins with third parties: it is amazing how readily some Bitcoiners who would never trust a banker in a suit are quite happy to trust their Bitcoin wealth to some anonymous outfit on the web, with no knowledge of who runs it or where it is located, and no recourse. In 2011, for example, the third largest wallet-guarding provider, Bitomat, claimed to have accidentally overwritten its entire Bitcoin wallet and its entire store of Bitcoin disappeared.

18 The botnet business is a sophisticated one, with a well-developed market for infections with a going rate in April 2013 of around $100 for every 1,000 infections. The market leader in this area is ZeroAccess, which a recent report labelled as the top Internet security threat in the first quarter of 2013: it was allegedly generating 100,000 infections a week in early 2013 and is said to have made $2.7 million in profit in 2012 from botnet mining alone.

and/or to manipulate the market for profit: attackers sell in an attempt to trigger a panic and then buy up Bitcoin afterwards at much lower prices. These attacks have been damaging – a DDoS attack on Mt. Gox on 3 April 2013 led to major disruption, a sharp fall in Bitcoin prices, and a lot of bad publicity – but Bitcoin exchanges have weathered these and other attacks and are becoming more experienced at handling them.[19]

A second use of botnets is to mine for Bitcoin. Botnets are a major problem for honest Bitcoin miners who lose revenue to them, and it is conceivable that botnets might be able to drive honest miners out of business due to their lower costs: the cost of operating a botnet boils down to the cost of infecting them, since the computer rental and electricity consumed are stolen, whereas an honest miner has to pay the full operating cost.[20] Were honest miners driven out of business, the entire Bitcoin industry would become criminalised, and the integrity of the market itself would be potentially undermined as honest players left and the market increasingly attracted unwelcome attention from law enforcement (Güring and Grigg 2011).

---

19 Mt. Gox has come in for considerable criticism because of weaknesses in its own security, but as new exchanges enter the market we can expect to see security standards improve and market prices become harder to manipulate or attack.

20 There are various Bitcoin mining calculators on the web, and these allow one to infer the profitability of both legitimate and botnet mining. Paganini (2013) offers some illustrative numbers for 24 April 2013 that suggest that a botnet with 1,000 bots would generate a monthly profit of $210. This profit rate is also directly scalable, so, for example, a botnet with 100,000 bots would generate a monthly profit of $21,000.

Fortunately, the problem of botnet mining seems to be correcting itself: professional miners are increasingly turning to custom-made chips known as Asics (Application-Specific Integrated Circuits) for mining purposes, and these are much faster than conventional desktop computers. Asic mining will then make botnet mining uncompetitive, and the problem should disappear.

Another threat is that from collusive behaviour. This threat was explicitly considered in the original design of the Bitcoin system. If a rogue node in the system were to give itself a larger reward than the protocol allows, other nodes are supposed to reject the attempt. Other nodes could collude but the difficulties of 'gaming' the system through collusion should increase as the network gets bigger and ultimately makes collusion impossible. However, Lee (2011) argues that collusion might be possible because a handful of clients is likely to account for the overwhelming majority of nodes at any one time. Lee suggests that a group of big players could then collude by changing the rules (for example, by awarding themselves 100 Bitcoins instead of 50 for winning a round). The nodes that enforce the original rules would then reject blocks with the higher rewards, but the rogue nodes would recognise each other's nodes and in so doing establish a rival Bitcoin network. The two networks would then compete, but in all likelihood one would soon dominate and become accepted as the 'real' Bitcoin network, in which case Bitcoin produced by the losing network would lose all their value.

This is a reasonable argument but, if it were correct, one presumes that rogue nodes should *already* have corrupted the system and created so much new Bitcoin that the currency would have hyperinflated by now – and this has not happened. I am therefore inclined to think that, though the Bitcoin network would have been vulnerable to threats from collusion in its earlier stages, it is probably now past the point where such threats could bring Bitcoin down.

Yet forks – cases of rival networks – *are* a problem, but appear to be a product of coding deficiencies rather than collusion. In the most widely reported case so far, a fork occurred on 11 March 2013, in which a miner using version 0.8.0 created a large amount of Bitcoin incompatible with earlier versions of the software. However, system administrators rapidly responded – large mining pools using 0.8.0 were asked to downgrade temporarily to 0.7 to kill off the 'illegitimate' fork. There was some minor disruption but within days a new version 0.8.1 was issued that fixed the software 'bug' that had enabled the rogue miner to create the fork in the first place.[21]

Such episodes illustrate, not so much the vulnerability of the Bitcoin network to forks and other threats, but rather its robustness and ability to handle them. The analogy here is with standard software in which problems are identified as they come up and system administrators issue upgrades to resolve them.[22,23]

---

21 The official Bitcoin report on this episode is available at https://en.bitcoin.it/wiki/BIP_50

22 Indeed, this is already what happens with the Bitcoin network: bugs are identified as they arise and cleaned up. A list of these problems and how they were resolved is given at https://en.bitcoin.it/wiki/Common_Vulnerabilities_and_Exposures.

23 Needless to say, there are also threats from the state: we will come to these presently.

Other threats of collusive behaviour have also been suggested. Lee (2011) suggests that key players might be able to build up power bases, leading to the cartelisation of the Bitcoin market and the emergence of controlling institutions with central-bank-like powers. Similarly, Grinberg (2012) suggests that Bitcoin's five-member development team – which is responsible for maintaining, debugging and improving the software – might take over the system and function like a Bitcoin central bank. Such arguments mirror earlier arguments (such as that of Goodhart 1989) that market forces would lead free banking to eventually give way to central banking. The response is twofold. While market structure and forms of self-regulation are already emerging in the Bitcoin market, the powers of large players are themselves limited by the market, by the threat of free entry and by the absence of legal compulsion. Thus, any market-based rules would be akin to club rules, and would be very different from the regulations imposed by modern central banks, which are of an altogether more sweeping nature and only made possible by state intervention and the underyling threats of state coercion. Secondly, the historical record indicates that modern central banking did not in fact evolve naturally via market forces, but via a long series of state interventions (see Dowd 1990). As for the Bitcoin market, there is no evidence that the development team have made any effort to take control of the Bitcoin system; on the contrary, their role has been limited to software improvement and firefighting.

The future of Bitcoin

It is interesting to speculate on how future Bitcoin prices might behave. Let us begin by considering a simplified textbook demand for money function that ignores the impact of the interest rate on money demand:[24]

$$M/P = \alpha Y^\beta \tag{1}$$

where M is the nominal demand for money, P is the price level, Y is real income as a proxy for the level of transactions, β is the income elasticity of demand, which empirical demand for money studies suggest might be in the region of about 0.5, and α is a normalising constant. In other words, if $\beta = 0.5$, the real demand for money (after adjusting for the price level) is proportionate to the square root of the level of real income.

This suggests a corresponding Bitcoin demand function of the form:

$$P^B M^B = \alpha Y^\beta \theta \tag{2}$$

where M^B is the demand for Bitcoin, P^B is the relative price of Bitcoin against goods and services (or the inverse of the price level measured in Bitcoin) and $0 \leq \theta \leq 1$ is the Bitcoin market share. Note also that the superscript 'B' denotes that the variables relate to Bitcoin; they are not powers.

The real demand for Bitcoin (the left-hand side of equation (2)) depends on the market share of Bitcoin together with the level of real income.

It is possible to use these equations to think about how the price of Bitcoin might change over time – especially in

---

24 The mathematics will be explained for the non-mathematical reader.

the long run when no more Bitcoin are produced. For example, if real economic growth were 2 per cent, β equalled 0.5 and the number of Bitcoin in circulation fell due to attrition, loss and so on, by 0.5 per cent per annum, then it is easy to show that the real price of Bitcoin (over and above the rise in price caused by inflation in the state currency) would rise by about 1.5 per cent per annum as long as the market share of Bitcoin remained approximately constant.

This implies that, if prices were measured in Bitcoin, we would have a long-run Bitcoin deflation rate of (about) 1.5 per cent. In sum, in this very long run – assuming Bitcoin ever got to it – goods prices in Bitcoin would be prone to deflation arising from the combination of economic growth and the Bitcoin attrition rate.[25] However, it could take a long time for the market share to stop growing and, until that happened, the price of Bitcoin would be rising by over 1.5 per cent a year and a Bitcoin price level would fall at a correspondingly faster rate – and it would fall even faster if the economic growth or attrition rates were higher than assumed.

The shorter-term cases are more complicated because we also have to consider a possibly changing Bitcoin market share and the impact of the rising supply of Bitcoin. In these cases, a rising market share will push up the price

---

25 It is interesting to note that this projected rate of increase in the Bitcoin price is not that far away from a plausible real interest rate and, under some asset price models, we would expect the price to rise with the real interest rate. Thus, two alternative approaches to the long-term behaviour of the price of Bitcoin give much the same order-of-magnitude answer.

of Bitcoin and the higher Bitcoin supply will work in the opposite direction. The analysis is complicated further because the growth of market share will depend on the supply of Bitcoin and possibly other elements in the equation (in the technical language, the market share is endogenous). The rate of growth is currently still high (about 7 per cent during 2013) but is falling rapidly and will soon fade out.

We can then envisage three main possibilities:

- The future growth rate of market share might be low, in which case the driving factor would be supply. We might then expect the (sterling) price of Bitcoin to fall, but at a decreasing rate as the rate of growth slows down. In other words, for a limited period, there will be Bitcoin inflation (a rise in the price of goods and services denominated in Bitcoin). In this case, the market would soon approach its longer-term equilibrium, but Bitcoin would have a very small market share.

- The future growth rate of market share might be high enough to make it the driving factor, in which case we might expect the price of Bitcoin to continue to trend upward. Moreover, if the growth rate of market share is high enough, we could get a situation where its rise in price was sufficiently high for sufficiently long to make Bitcoin the object of a speculative bubble or bubble–bust cycle: people rush into Bitcoin as an investment and the market later falls, possibly to recover and repeat the experience again and again.

Indeed, such a scenario would appear to be a good description of the history of the Bitcoin market to date.

- Something might happen to destroy the demand for Bitcoin altogether. This might happen in response to a particularly severe market bust or (more likely) if something were to happen to compromise the integrity of the Bitcoin market or if the government or some competitor currency were eventually able to stamp or drive Bitcoin out.

The fact that none of these possibilities can easily be ruled out tells us that the future Bitcoin market is highly unpredictable.

The message is that, although the Bitcoin system produces a highly predictable *supply* of money, the *demand* is very unpredictable – and there is nothing in the Bitcoin system to stabilise it.

From the point of view of Bitcoin price stability, the root problem is a fundamental and inescapable tension between the following three factors:

- The inelastic Bitcoin supply schedule and the fact that supply is not responsive to demand.
- Achieving significant take-up relative to existing currencies.
- Avoiding a rate of price increase that would likely trigger a bubble or bubble-bust cycle.

Given the inelastic supply, if there is a significant take-up of Bitcoin a bubble–bust cycle is very much a possibility.

Put differently, given the way Bitcoin is designed, a major increase in demand is impossible without a corresponding increase in the Bitcoin price.

There is a related problem. A sharp rise in the price of Bitcoin means a sharp fall in the price of anything denominated in Bitcoin, i.e. hyper-deflation. In this case, many people would be reluctant to buy anything with Bitcoin: the temptation would be to hoard Bitcoin instead. Conversely, if Bitcoin prices fell, people would be reluctant to acquire Bitcoin for fear that the currency might soon become worthless. To quote Willard Foxton in the *Daily Telegraph*:

> As an economy where Bitcoin was the main currency, Silk Road recently went through a hyper-deflation almost unprecedented in economics. Following the recent surges in the value of Bitcoin, people have been selling less and less, initially because the value of the Bitcoins was going up so fast people were unwilling to part with them; then, once the Bitcoin price started crashing, dealers were unwilling to part with valuable drugs for Bitcoins worth who-knows-what.

This illustrates how major volatility in the price of Bitcoin can seriously impact on its ability to perform its medium of exchange function – but even so the market still continued to operate.

Returning to the issue of the future of Bitcoin, in the short to medium term – barring a major upset – the most likely scenario for the Bitcoin market is more of the same but with the market lurching towards maturity. The Bitcoin market will continue to grow, but in a fitful manner with one boom–bust cycle after another before settling down as the growing size of the market makes manipulative attacks more difficult and the exchanges' risk management continues to improve.

In the long run, is Bitcoin dead?

Will Bitcoin grow to displace conventional currency? Probably, it will not. However, to focus on the size of the Bitcoin market relative to conventional currency is to miss the main point. The significance of Bitcoin lies not in its size but in its nature, and in particular its novelty and the fact that it is ideally suited to a niche market driven by legal restrictions. In other words, a key reason people demand Bitcoin is to do things they are not legally permitted to do, whether that is to buy illicit drugs, launder money, evade exchange controls or taxes, or hide their wealth. As long as the 'underground' economy continues to grow so, too, will the demand for Bitcoin and other currencies that service that economy.

This creates a delightful irony: the more the state restricts or prohibits forms of commerce, the more the Bitcoin market will thrive as individuals use it to evade state control: thus, it is the state itself that is the main driving factor behind the growth of the Bitcoin market.[26]

---

26 There is also an obvious corollary: if the state really wants to get rid of Bitcoin, it should eliminate the state controls that feed it, for example, if the state ended the wars on drugs and on terror, reduced taxes, ended policies of financial repression and re-established the privacy of individuals' personal financial information.

Nonetheless, in the longer run, Bitcoin is almost certain to fail – and this is no bad thing. The pioneers in any industry are rarely the ones who last: who remembers Betamax from the early days of the video industry? Bitcoin might have been the first successful cryptocurrency, but it is not yet clear whether being the first mover in this area is even an advantage in the longer term. After all, any major design flaws in the Bitcoin model are set in concrete and competitors can learn from them. The cryptocurrency market is also an open one and a considerable number of new competitors have already entered the field. These include, among others, Litecoin, Namecoin, PPCoin, Freicoin, Ripple, Primecoin, Terracoin and Feathercoin.[27] Most of these will probably soon fail, but, as competition in the market develops, no one can predict which cryptocurrencies will be best suited to the market and achieve long-run success. For what it's worth, the author's guess is that Bitcoin will eventually be displaced by other cryptocurrencies with superior features.

The ideal – one is tempted to say, the gold standard in this area – would be one or more cryptocurrencies that were able to achieve stable purchasing power through elastic but fully automatic and hence non-discretionary supply schedules when real demand changes, and which

---

27 An informal overview of some of these alternative currencies is provided by Bradbury (2013), but hard details are difficult to find. In terms of market share, however, these new cryptocurrencies are totally dwarfed by Bitcoin, which has at least 99.9 per cent of the market. The next biggest is Litecoin with a market share of 0.05 per cent, if that, and the others are much smaller still.

also have the ability to maintain state-of-the-art security. Going further, the ultimate possibility for those who believe in private money is that cryptocurrencies might eventually become so widely accepted that they drive government currencies out of circulation and expel the government from the monetary system once and for all.

The broader implications of cryptocurrency are extremely profound. The key issues here are well worth dwelling on:

- The freedom of the individual to trade, and
- The freedom of the individual to accumulate, move and protect his or her financial wealth – in other words, financial freedom.

Intertwined with these are deep moral questions and, needless to say, the government response. The root issue is the individual versus the state.

Free trade: the Silk Road

The best example of the freedom-to-trade issue is Silk Road.[1] As noted already, this is an anonymous online exchange

---

1   Silk Road was hosted by a colourful character who went by the name Dread Pirate Roberts (or DPR) after the hero in *The Princess Bride*. Judging by his postings on Silk Road, DPR is an eloquent anarcho-capitalist with an excellent grasp of Austrian economics and an admiration for Ron Paul; he also delights in defying the

system that uses Bitcoin to enable users to purchase a great variety of goods, mainly illegal drugs.[2] There are two main aspects of how Silk Road worked that need to be understood. The first, familiar from, for example, eBay, is that it used a reputation-based trading system: potential buyers are naturally assumed to distrust sellers whom they do not know, but could check their ratings from previous customers and then transact with those who had good ratings. Sellers had an incentive to promote and maintain a good reputation, and this discouraged them from cheating their customers. The reviews on the website indicated that this system worked, even if there was the odd dispute between one party and another. Buyers were further reassured by an escrow system in which payments were handed over to a trusted middleman until delivery had been confirmed, and by a dispute resolution procedure with missing packages qualifying for partial refunds. The second key feature is that it made use of Tor (short for 'The onion ring' or 'The onion router'), a network and associated software that

government. An example of his unwillingness to compromise is his position on drug legalisation: he is against because it would give the government more control over the drugs business.

2 Despite its notoriety, there are some things that could not be bought on Silk Road. One is child pornography, which had always been banned; another is illegal weapons. Initially, weapons were available but the drug dealers on the site were unhappy about the presence of arms dealers, which they feared would bring unwanted attention from law enforcement agencies. In response, a dedicated weapons site known as the Armory was spun off from Silk Road, but this was closed down a few months later because it was not sufficiently profitable.

allows anonymous web browsing. The user would connect to Silk Road using an onion URL, and the Tor software would then connect the user through the Tor network to a hidden server whose location was impossible to find.

Judging by their reviews on its website, customers seemed satisfied with their purchases. One customer was reported as having used it to buy ten tabs of quality LSD delivered directly to his home in the US courtesy of the US Post Office (Chen 2011). Prices were higher than on the street, but the product and service were superior: home delivery, better quality assurance, less aggravation, and so on.

After it was launched, word about Silk Road spread quickly across the dark web. Then, on 1 June 2011, came an article in the *Gawker* and the story went viral. Silk Road was being described as the 'Amazon.com of illegal drugs' and a couple of days later Senator Charles Schumer called on the government agencies to shut it down. He said:

> Literally, it allows buyers and users to sell illegal drugs online, including heroin, cocaine, and meth, and users do sell by hiding their identities through a program that makes them virtually untraceable ... It's a certifiable one-stop shop for illegal drugs that represents the most brazen attempt to peddle drugs online that we have ever seen. It's more brazen than anything else by light years.
>
> (Associated Press 2011)

This blaze of publicity must have served as a powerful endorsement, as it led to a dramatic increase in the website's activity and a sharp increase in the price of Bitcoin.[3]

---

3 End-of-day prices on Mt. Gox jumped from $8.88 on 30 May to $29.58 ten days later.

Exactly how the US government was supposed to shut down an untraceable trading network using an untraceable digital currency, however, the senator did not say.

Silk Road had some major attractions beyond giving individuals trading the satisfaction of defying the government. One supporter described it as the 'truly *free* market' that:

> [h]ackers, anarchists, and criminals have been dreaming about ... since forever. Where you can turn on your computer, browse the web anonymously, make an untraceable cash-like transaction, and have a product in your hands, regardless of what any government or authority decides. We're at a new point in history.
>
> (Anonymous 2012)

He went on to comment that the Silk Road makes buying things that can get you thrown into a prison cell for a decade or so, incredibly smooth and simple.

He then described a post on the Silk Road forum by two people arguing over a deal that had gone wrong. One of them claimed to have been cheated and started threatening the other, but other people on the forum made fun of him and told him to stop making a fool of himself: threats were pointless because everyone was anonymous and anonymity made violence impossible. The anonymous writer, above, then continued:

> [This] showed how successful Silk Road really is. It makes drug buying and selling so smooth that it's easy to forget how violent drug dealers can be ... Thanks to decentralization and powerful encryption, we're able to operate in a

digital world that is almost free from prohibition and the violence it causes...

This goes beyond people trying to get around laws and use the Internet to commit crime. This goes beyond that nasty scar on the face of human history, the 'war on drugs.' This is about *real* freedom. Freedom from violence, from arbitrary morals and law, from corrupt centralized authorities, and from centralization altogether. While Silk Road and Bitcoin may fade or be crushed by their enemies, we've seen what free, leaderless systems can do. You can only chop off so many heads.

This is the future.[4]

In the nearly two years following, Silk Road would seem to have gone from strength to strength. A glitch occurred in early June 2013 when the site went off-line for two weeks: this prompted rumours that DPR had been caught or had run off with the site's deposits, that the site had come under attack, and so forth. However, it turned out that the volume of business had been growing so fast that the infrastructure had been overloaded – Silk Road had been a victim of its own success – and a full redeployment of the entire system was needed to enhance its capacity and improve security.

For users of illegal exchange markets, the key to success is to be very careful with personal security, and the weakest link in the security chain is delivery. As one journalist noted, 'one can expect that sooner or later folks who buy drugs at the [Silk Road] site will be seeing something

---

4 The quotation has been edited slightly to maintain a more polite form of language.

other than a friendly UPS man at their door' (Cartier 2011). One can also imagine law enforcement agencies setting up sting operations, for example. One blogger went further and suggested that the problem with Silk Road was that it was:

> Totally anonymous, except that you have to turn in a shipping address. So the DEA sets up a front account and starts selling piddly amounts of drugs – a few hits of acid here, a few ecstasy pills there. Once they've built up a good reputation, they start posting huge sales, like 'intent-to-distribute-go-away-forever' amounts. The buyers get busted and the DEA looks like a hero. This continues until the front account gets busted.

Moreover, even the anonymity of Bitcoin itself cannot be taken for granted. When the *Gawker* article came out, Jeff Garzik, a member of the Bitcoin core development team, went on record to say that because of Bitcoin's public log – even though the identities of all parties are anonymous – it might still be possible for law enforcement agencies to parse the transaction flow and track down users in the same way that they can detect suspicious money flows and Internet chatter: 'Attempting major illicit transactions with bitcoin, given existing statistical analysis techniques deployed in the field by law enforcement, is pretty damned dumb,' he wrote (quoted in Cartier 2011).

This cautionary note was confirmed by Andy Greenberg (2013): he outlined an experiment in which he and his colleagues at Forbes had carried out some black market transactions and hired Sarah Meiklejohn from the University of California, San Diego, to try to track them down. Her investigation revealed that their online drug buys were 'visible to practically anyone who took the time to look.' A more detailed investigation showed that snooping in the blockchain can often uncover who owns which Bitcoin addresses (Meiklejohn et al. 2013). However, the Forbes experiment also showed there were limits to this traceability. As Greenberg explains:

> Bitcoin users seeking privacy should be careful about revealing their addresses in public or using subpoenable Bitcoin services like Coinbase that might connect their Bitcoin addresses and real names. If we had taken the extra consideration of shuffling our bitcoin expenditures through other addresses with desktop-based wallet software, or gone to the further effort of sending them through a bitcoin 'laundry service' such as Bitlaundry, Bitmix or Bitcoinlaundry, tracing them would have become much harder or even impossible.

Again, the plain fact is that if you use Bitcoin to engage in illegal transactions you have to be very careful about your personal security. Most users are not.

But even average users pose major problems for law enforcement and law enforcement themselves do not rate their own chances highly. A Federal Bureau of Investigation (FBI) report leaked online in May 2012 indicated that they were clearly struggling; it also revealed that the FBI had only 'medium confidence' that it could 'in some cases' identify criminals using Bitcoin on the black market. However, some lines of attack are surely obvious: they can intensify efforts to screen for suspicious parcels; they can follow the money and chase suspicious cash flows; they can mount sting operations; they can monitor Bitcoin exchanges; they can target individuals and such like.[5] The appropriate defensive strategies are equally obvious.

The government then had a stroke of luck when, on 3 October 2013, somebody believed to be DPR was caught. This person turned out to be 29-year-old Ross Ulbricht operating out of a coffee shop in San Francisco. They caught him through a combination of good luck and carelessness on his part.[6] After his arrest, the government alleged he had generated sales of $1.2 billion on Silk Road and had made a personal profit in the neighbourhood of $100 mil-

---

5   One success for law enforcement came from a major international effort known as Operation Adam Bomb that led to the closing down in April 2011 of another dark web market outfit called the Farmer's Market, which sold all manner of illegal merchandise. The US Department of Justice was quick to hail this a major success. The reality, however, was that Farmer's Market was insignificant. Its competitors had long outgrown it and it made mistakes that allowed the government to seize email and payment details. Since then, other sites have stepped into its place and the online black market continues to boom.

6   In July 2013, the FBI got a break when Canadian border control randomly inspected a package that contained a number of fake passports and identities all addressed to Ulbricht. Homeland Security duly visited him at his San Francisco address and he was now on their radar. He made a number of mistakes, including using his real photo on the fake identities, using his real name on social media when asking about hidden sites, talking too much on social media and inadvertently hiring an undercover investigator to carry out a hit, or so it is alleged. The FBI was then able to connect him to Silk Road and he was duly arrested.

lion depending on how his Bitcoin wealth was valued. He is now in custody awaiting trial on charges of conspiracy to traffic narcotics, hack computers and launder money and of soliciting murder for hire.[7] The site itself was seized and shut down.

But Silk Road wasn't down for long: within days a number of outfits were vying with each other to set up Silk Road 2.0. One insider commented that he had counted at least five publicly stated projects with the said aim of becoming 'Silk Road 2.0' and many more gathering information and building alliances. This commentator pondered:

> And this is what Law Enforcement is now parading as a victory? Over two years of investigation, millions of dollars spent and for what so that a couple of armchair programmers can build it again in a couple of days…

There is also a-learning-from-mistakes process going on. Each bust works as evolutionary pressure, weeding out the weaker sites and teaching the others what to avoid. Cut one head off, and new ones will take its place: Silk Road 2.0 is already up and operating at http://silkroad5v7dywlc.onion.[8]

---

7   It was alleged that he had solicited and paid for the murder of a Canadian Silk Road user named FriendlyChemist, who had supposedly tried to extort money from him by threatening to reveal the identities of thousands of the site's users.

8   It is sometimes suggested in discussions of illegal exchanges that the government could close them down by attacking the Tor itself. There are, however, two big problems with such a proposal. The first is moral: whatever one thinks of Silk Road, the Tor is also used

Financial freedom

The implications of Bitcoin and associated innovations go much further than merely facilitating the purchase of illegal commodities. A good starting point is to note that the system has no regard for international borders and can be used by anyone with access to the Internet. As one blogger put it:

> As long as my encrypted [Bitcoin] wallet exists somewhere in the world, such as on an email account, I can walk across national borders with nothing on me and retrieve my wealth from anywhere in the world with an Internet connection.[9]

This gives Bitcoin great potential as an internationally mobile store of value that offers a high degree of security

---

by many other groups whose activities arouse much sympathy, such as Arab Spring bloggers and Chinese and Iranian dissidents. The second is practical: the Tor and similar networks are distributed – that is, decentralised – and there is no obvious way in which government can close them down. There is a major irony here, as it was the US government that developed the Tor in the first place to protect the secrecy of intelligence communications. It then privatised it and continues to support it through the State Department's Internet freedom budget. Thus, in a splendid illustration of the law of unintended consequences – not to mention one hand of government not knowing what the other is doing – the very cryptographic technology that the government developed to protect its secrecy escaped from their control and is now being used to protect the secrecy of the private sector against the government itself.

9 http://detlevschlichter.com/2011/06/bitcoin-gold-and-the-demise -of-fiat-money

against predatory governments and unsafe banks – thus fulfilling but also extending the role that Swiss bank accounts used to fill before Swiss banks were required to 'co-operate' with US and other law enforcement agencies.

Indeed, it is interesting to note how much things have changed in this respect. What is now regarded as rebellious and anarchic was perfectly normal 100 years ago. As A. J. P. Taylor (1965) put it:

> Until August 1914 a sensible, law-abiding Englishman could pass through life and hardly notice the existence of the state, beyond the post office and the policeman ... He could travel abroad or leave his country for ever without a passport or any sort of official permission. He could exchange his money for any other currency without restriction or limit. ... For that matter, a foreigner could spend his life in this country without permit and without informing the police ... Substantial householders were occasionally called on for jury service. Otherwise, only those helped the state who wished to do so.

Bitcoin allows people to undertake activities that were regarded as natural rights but which have increasingly become regulated activities or activities that the state observes.

Possible uses for such an internationally mobile medium include investing wealth safely abroad, circumventing exchange and capital controls, anonymous money transfer (including money laundering) and tax avoidance and evasion. Three diverse examples illustrate the point.

The first is the right to gamble. The Unlawful Internet Gambling Enforcement Act of 2006 currently allows US residents to access online gambling and betting sites, but does not allow residents to place bets on them. It also requires payments systems to block any such transactions. However, US residents minded to do so can place bets on any of these sites provided the sites accept Bitcoin. A good example is the Bitcoin gambling site Satoshdice: this was an Internet sensation and within weeks of its launch in April 2012 was said to be accounting for more Bitcoin transactions than all other uses combined.[10]

A second is the right to make payments to whomsoever one wishes – and in particular, to outfits of which the government disapproves. The outstanding example is Wikileaks. Following a massive release of secret US diplomatic cables by Wikileaks in November 2010, the US government orchestrated an illegal financial blockade by pressuring major payments providers such as Visa, Mastercard, Bank of America and PayPal to block payments to Wikileaks and/or freeze the group's accounts so it could not access funds already collected. Wikileaks were, however, able to circumvent this blockade by accepting payments in Bitcoin. To quote Jon Matonis (2012):

> It used to be that people had secrets and the government was transparent; now it's the people that lack privacy and the government has secrets. Freedom of payments is an extension of financial privacy and digital cash-like

---

10 This site was closed to US residents in May 2013 – presumably in response to US government pressure – but there are other sites still available and doubtless new ones will continue to emerge to meet the demand.

transactions without financial intermediaries become a critical piece of that foundation. Money was never intended to act as a form of identity tracking or payments restriction and this is why the option for anonymous and untraceable transactions is so vital as society moves to a world of digital currency...

To those who don't support freedom of payments, consider this financial blockade invoked in the name of political correctness before you dismiss the inherent value of a non-political unit of account and of a decentralized medium of exchange. It should be offensive to most free-minded people that *you* are not the final arbiter of how and where you spend your money. Bitcoin restores the balance. [His emphasis][11]

A third is to make investments free of government control. This may be done to evade or avoid taxes on investment returns or capital gains or for other reasons. As things currently stand, individuals who are careful about security can invest their wealth in Bitcoin and so evade any taxes they would normally be liable for or avoid taxes perfectly legally in some circumstances. However, they then face the problem of being exposed to Bitcoin price risk. The natural solution is to hedge their Bitcoin wealth: a US domiciled investor might want to hedge against the

---

11 The standard excuse is that such controls are needed to counter terrorism. However, we should put this threat into perspective. A recent article in *The Atlantic* examined this issue and concluded that Americans were as likely to be killed by their own furniture (TV sets falling onto them, etc.) as by terrorists. The terrorist argument, if accepted, also opens up a thin end of the wedge that would sanction the government being able to do anything it wishes and this is exactly what we see. But I digress.

risk that Bitcoin could fall against the US dollar, and the problem is that the hedge position might not be anonymous, since a typical US dollar hedge would be with a 'regular' broker or exchange. So what is needed here is to be able to anonymously acquire Bitcoin derivatives, the values of which will fluctuate with the US dollar/Bitcoin exchange rate. One can imagine these soon becoming available and already there is a new service, Open Transactions,[12] that offers users the opportunity to use Bitcoin to acquire anonymous positions denominated in other currencies, and these should enable Bitcoin investors to hedge their Bitcoin positions anonymously. Widespread tax evasion of this sort would put pressure on governments worldwide to reduce tax rates, and in doing so, reduce the incentive to evade tax in the first place.

Implicit in the above is the ability of Bitcoin to enable individuals to protect their wealth. This, in turn, is intimately related to the financial privacy that was once provided by bank secrecy laws. As Martin Hutchinson recently wrote (Hutchinson 2013), bank secrecy is no less than a key civil liberty. He then elaborates:

> The first bank secrecy law was written by Switzerland in 1934 and played a vital role in enabling at least some German Jews to preserve both their lives and their assets during the horrors of World War II. The 'key civil liberty' aspect of bank secrecy laws thus cannot be dismissed. While we will hopefully never again have a regime as evil as the Nazis, there are plenty of regimes around the world

---

12 https://github.com/FellowTraveler/Open-Transactions

that oppress their subjects, and those subjects need an asset bolt-hole where they can preserve their wealth while they emigrate or simply decide to wait for better times.

It's not surprising that there were no bank secrecy laws before 1934. The London merchant banks and private banks of the 19th century would have binned immediately a demand from any government other than Britain's for their customers' records. Numerous dissidents such as Louis Napoleon (the future Napoleon III) and Lajos Kossuth, the Hungarian revolutionary, could keep their money in London entirely without fear of expropriation for that reason. As for Britain itself, with income tax at less than 5% for most of the nineteenth century there was no great incentive for tax evasion, although accounts were occasionally frozen in fraud cases.

After World War II ... Britain had exchange controls until 1979, while its governments ... pursued highly repressive policies, with top rates of tax above 90% for almost the entire period, interest rates around or below the rate of inflation, and inflation itself eroding the real value of savings. It's ... not surprising that even in that law-abiding society, many people found ways to get their money out of Britain's closed economy and into the safe hands of a Swiss or Channel Islands bank.[13]

---

13 In the EU, the last country holding out to protect bank secrecy is Austria, which passed bank secrecy legislation in 1978 as part of a belated effort to get some of Switzerland's business. To quote Hutchinson again:

> It was said to be tighter than Swiss legislation, because you never needed to give your real name, merely show the nationality of your passport. If you said your name was Mickey Mouse, the bank staff would accept this, and when you visited the bank cheerfully greet you with 'Gruss Gott, Doktor Maus!'

Thus, Bitcoin helps to fill the role once provided by bank secrecy laws.

There is no easy way in which the government can prevent these and similar uses of Bitcoin to evade government control. The combination of anonymity and independence means that governments cannot bring down Bitcoin by conventional methods, although they may occasionally catch individuals and organisations that are careless. They cannot bring Bitcoin down by taking down particular individuals or organisations because the system is not dependent on any individual or organisation: there is no single point of failure. They could shut down the Bitcoin website Bitcoin.org or harass individual exchanges such as Mt. Gox, but this wouldn't make much difference and the Bitcoin community would carry on regardless.[14] Governments would instead have to take out the whole Bitcoin community and they cannot do that because they cannot identify who the Bitcoin community might be – and they cannot (yet) spy on everyone, although recent revelations about

---

14 Indeed, the government has already made several lame attempts to harass Bitcoin organisations. In May 2013, the Department of Homeland Security seized Mt. Gox's Dwolla electronic payments account because of alleged paperwork violations, and in June the California Department of Financial Institutions issued 'cease and desist' orders against the Bitcoin Foundation on the spurious grounds that it was involved in transferring money, which it was not. This latter operation in particular was the subject of considerable ridicule on the blogosphere.

PRISM suggest that they are making major efforts to do exactly that.[15]

We should also put governmental responses into context. For a long time now, it has been clear that these are not so much responses to breaches of specific laws, but a sustained attack on freedom itself. Freedoms have been subject to more and more exceptions: there were exceptions to counter money laundering, terrorism, offshore financial centres that offered less onerous legal regimes (such as lower tax rates), payments to whistle blowers and organisations on government blacklists and so on. In the US, people used to be free to do almost anything; now they are free to do anything except what is on a long and growing government list of what they can't do.[16] We have gone

---

15 We wouldn't even know about much of this activity if it were not for whistle blowers such as Wikileaks and Ed Snowden. There are many ways in which this surveillance activity is increasing. An article in *Wired* last year revealed that the US government is building a large spy centre in Bluffdale, Utah – so large, in fact, that once finished, the facility will be five times larger than the Capitol. Its purpose is to intercept, decipher, analyse and store vast chunks of the world's communications. It would collect all forms of communication, including the complete contents of private emails, mobile phone calls and Internet searches, as well as personal data trails such as parking receipts, travel itineraries, purchases, and other digital 'pocket litter' – in short, it will collect everything. As an official involved admitted, 'everyone is a target'. Such efforts violate the Fourth Amendment's prohibition against mass searches and seizures related to the unspecified crimes of unnamed persons.

16 Nor is the US government alone in this respect. The UK government recently proposed a law that would allow it to monitor all Internet traffic through the UK, and it is already a criminal offence to refuse to hand over passwords when government officials demand them.

from a situation where privacy – including financial privacy – was respected, to one where it is now openly repudiated, not just in the name of some allegedly greater good (such as the war against terror or whatever) but just openly repudiated.

But, because of strong cryptography, the balance of power is swinging back towards the individual and there is not much that the state can do to stop it. Censorship, prohibition, oppressive taxes, financial repression and repression generally, will all be undermined as people increasingly escape into the cyphersphere where they can operate freely away from government harassment. As Tim May wrote in his Crypto-Anarchist Manifesto as long ago as 1988:

> A specter is haunting the world, the specter of crypto-anarchy.
> Computer technology is on the verge of providing the ability for individuals and groups to communicate and interact with each other in a totally anonymous manner. Two persons may exchange messages, conduct business,

---

However, UK residents can protect the privacy of their Internet activities by using a Tor browser (this is downloadable for free at https://www.torproject.org/download/download) and by making sure that they follow the security advice given by the authors of the Tor software. As for the requirement to surrender passwords, this can be circumvented using automatic rekeying of secure channels: this renders the old keys inaccessible, so making it impossible for the user to disclose the old key even if they were willing to do so. And of course individuals can use cryptography to hide the existence of encrypted messages so law enforcement agencies cannot find them in the first place.

and negotiate electronic contracts without ever knowing the True Name, or legal identity, of the other. Interactions over networks will be untraceable, via extensive re-routing of encrypted packets and tamper-proof boxes which implement cryptographic protocols with nearly perfect assurance against any tampering. Reputations will be of central importance, far more important in dealings than even the credit ratings of today. These developments will alter completely the nature of government regulation, the ability to tax and control economic interactions, the ability to keep information secret, and will even alter the nature of trust and reputation.

The State will of course try to slow or halt the spread of this technology, citing national security concerns, use of the technology by drug dealers and tax evaders, and fears of societal disintegration. Many of these concerns will be valid; crypto anarchy will allow national secrets to be traded freely and will allow illicit and stolen materials to be traded. ... But this will not halt the spread of crypto anarchy.

6   CONCLUSIONS

Contemporary private money and the functions of money

The modern private monies considered here are radical in their nature. To displace existing state currency they not only have to perform the basic functions of money at least as well as state money, they probably also need qualities that transcend the way in which state money works. The network benefits from the use of a single money are substantial and the costs of changing from one network to another would be very large. Hence, for new private monies to achieve a significant market share, they have to demonstrate substantial benefits. Let us consider this issue from the perspective of the traditional functions of money.

Money is expected to provide a measure of value or unit of account. It would seem that the new private monies do achieve this function, either by having their own denomination (for example, Bitcoin) or by being denominated relative to an existing unit of account (for example, Liberty Dollar). However, new monies do not have any obvious advantage over existing monies in this respect.

Money should be effective as a medium of exchange. To fulfil this purpose, it has to be sufficiently widely acceptable. However, money does not have to be generally acceptable across the whole population to be useful as a medium of exchange. It is true that there is a cost of using two currencies if one of those currencies is not generally acceptable (potential exchange costs and forgone interest costs of holding more cash, for example), but these are probably not especially significant. It is clear that Bitcoin has become acceptable for transactions in growing but mostly niche markets; for their part, the Liberty Dollar and e-gold achieved considerable market take-up but did not have the opportunity to become more widely acceptable because of government action taken against them. The regulatory risk attached to private monies is thus clearly substantial, though we can expect mechanisms of avoiding such risk to be increasingly important features of new forms of money – and the ability to evade such risk is of course one of the main attractions of Bitcoin.

Thirdly, money should be a reasonable store of value. State money has not fulfilled this function well in the last eight decades at least.[1] Before World War II, UK inflation history had been reasonably good for nearly 300 years, much of which was spent on a metallic gold standard. Those new private monies that are based on gold can be expected to be a better long-term store of value than state

---

1   In the 2014 budget, the Chancellor of the Exchequer, George Osborne, announced the adoption of a new pound coin from 2017 with a very similar design to the pre-decimal three-penny bit first issued in 1937. As it happens, one pound in 2017 will buy only slightly more than a three-penny bit (equivalent to 1.25 decimal pence) would have bought in 1937.

money, even if their value denominated in state currency might fluctuate from time to time. It is notable in this context that each of the three private monetary systems we have considered also imposes discipline on the over-issue of money, a discipline that is conspicuously lacking in contemporary government monetary systems. I would suggest that this discipline is a central reason for the success that the private monetary systems have hitherto achieved.

Fourthly, modern private monies can also be used as a standard for deferred payments, as long as creditor and debtor are willing to accept the price fluctuations of private money relative to state money.

These case studies of contemporary private monetary systems indicate beyond any doubt that the demand for private money is very much alive and well – and private monetary systems have been successful so far because the money they provide is superior to that provided by the state, at least for certain purposes. They also demonstrate that any particular money does not have to have a monopoly (whether private or state) to achieve success in the marketplace: there is no 'need' for any monopoly in money.

These private monetary systems – the Liberty Dollar and e-gold more obviously, but Bitcoin implicitly with its gold-like supply schedule – also point to the continuing allure of gold. The attraction of gold should hardly be a surprise given the record of fiat money since the last link to gold was cut in 1971. Since then, the US dollar has lost almost 85 per cent of its purchasing power even by official government statistics; for its part, sterling has lost 98 per cent of its value over the last century since the abandonment of the 'High Gold Standard' that existed before World War I.

Regulation of contemporary private monies

The experience of contemporary private monetary systems shows that the only regulation they need is that by the market itself: in the provision of money as with the provision of other goods and services, the best outcomes are achieved by free competition. It is therefore important that more widespread adoption of private monies is not inhibited by the state. Such a response by the state would reduce consumer choice, reduce the competitive pressure on the state to maintain the quality of its currency and undermine financial freedom.

Competition against the central bank should therefore be welcomed, not least as it would pressure the central bank to improve the quality of the currency it provides. With this objective in mind, governments should consider eliminating any and all regulatory or legal obstacles to the use of private monies. One fairly obvious reform would be to repeal repressive regulation against private currency – such as the current US prohibition against the private issue of coins. A second useful reform would be to ensure that courts will enforce contracts made in any currency, private, official or foreign, so long as the parties involved have entered into them freely. Thirdly, transactions in any private or foreign currency should not be put at any tax disadvantage relative to transactions in the local official currency: the guiding principle should be a level playing field.

Note, too, that this would also imply the abolition of legal tender, by which parties to contracts can be compelled to accept a currency they would not freely choose. The principle of a level playing field also implies that the government itself should be willing to accept private monies in tax payments, should those monies become well established.

The worst policy response to the challenges posed by private money is to try to suppress it. Above all, we need to move away from the medieval attitude that the issue of any form of money is a state prerogative.

Cryptocurrencies and the transformation of society?

The most radical and far-reaching private monetary systems are the cryptocurrencies. At the broadest level and whatever its limitations and eventual fate, Bitcoin reminds us yet again of the ability of the private sector to produce astonishing innovations that are almost impossible to anticipate. To start with, the very existence of Bitcoin proves that anyone can create money that other people will accept using a computer that takes as its only inputs an algorithm and computing power. This new currency is similar to a commodity money, such as gold, in so far as it is costly to produce and inelastic in supply.

Bitcoin is truly radical in a number of other respects too. It is the first currency ever to achieve take-off despite having no commodity value. In this it differs from modern fiat currencies that also have no commodity value but which started off as convertible currencies and had the commodity link later severed. Bitcoin also differs from conventional note and deposit money in that it can in no way be construed as debt. Another breakthrough is that Bitcoin provides a novel solution to the trust problem: instead of relying on any individual or organisation, it achieves trust using a peer-to-peer network. Furthermore, once it was up and running, Bitcoin became independent of any individuals or organisations and can therefore continue without them – it has no single point of failure – and this makes it very hard to shut down. Finally, Bitcoin has the potential to achieve a very high degree of anonymity. These features open up almost unimaginable possibilities for private parties to free themselves from state control – to buy illegal drugs, engage in illegal forms of gambling, evade taxes, protect their wealth from the government, and so on. This, in turn, raises profound issues of an emerging spontaneous social order, in particular, the prospect of a crypto-anarchic society in which there is no longer any government role in the monetary system and, potentially, no government at all.

REFERENCES

Anonymous (2011) Silk Road: the Amazon.com of illegal drugs. *The Week*, 2 June.

Anonymous (2012) Silk Road: a vicious blow to the war on drugs. *The Austin Cut*, 2 January. (http://austincut.com/2012/01/silk-road-a-vicious-blow-to-the-war-on-drugs/)

Associated Press (2011) Schumer pushes to shut down online drug marketplace. NBC New York, 5 June. (http://www.nbcnewyork.com/news/local/Schumer-Calls-on-Feds-to-Shut-Down-Online-Drug-Marketplace-123187958.html)

Ball, J. (2013) Bitcoin will continue to function beyond the reach of government and law. *The Guardian*, 30 May.

Barnard, B. W. (1917) The use of private tokens for money in the United States. *Quarterly Journal of Economics* 31(4): 617–26.

Baxendale, T. (2011) Reforming fractional reserve banking. Posting on the Cobden Centre website, 8 March 2013. (This is the author's expert testimony to Ron Paul's Monetary Policy Anthology.) (http://www.cobdencentre.org/author/tbaxendale/#)

Bradbury, D. (2013) Bitcoin's successors: from Litecoin to Freicoin and onwards. *The Guardian*, 25 June.

Brough, W. (1898) *Open Mints and Free Banking*. New York: Putnam.

Chen, A. (2011) The underground website where you can buy any drug imaginable, 1 June. (http://gawker.com/5805928/the-underground-website-where-you-can-buy-any-drug-imaginable)

Cartier, C. (2011) 'Silk Road' website is the Amazon of the illegal-drug market. *Seattle Weekly News*, 1 June.

Chetson, D. (2011) Relevant conduct and federal sentencing. The Chetson Firm, PLLC, 3 December. (http://www.chetson. com/2011/12/relevant-conduct-and-federal-sentencing/)

Connolly, K. and Grandjean, G. (2013) Bitcoin: the Berlin streets where you can shop with virtual currency. *The Guardian*, 26 April.

Crispin, N. (2012) Travelling the Silk Road: a measurement analysis of a large anonymous online marketplace. Carnegie Mellon INI/CyLab, Working Paper, 1 August.

Dowd, K. (1990) Did central banks evolve naturally? A review essay of Charles Goodhart's *The Evolution of Central Banks*. *Scottish Journal of Political Economy* 37(1): 96–104.

Foxton, W. (2013) The online drug marketplace Silk Road is collapsing – did hackers, government or Bitcoin kill it? *The Daily Telegraph*, 1 May.

Franklin, O. (2013) Unravelling the dark web. *GQ*, February.

Goodhart, C. (1988) *The Evolution of Central Banks*. Cambridge, MA: MIT Press.

Greenberg, A. (2013) Follow the Bitcoins: how we got busted buying drugs on Silk Road's black market. *Forbes*, 5 September.

Grinberg, R. (2012) Bitcoin: an innovative alternative digital currency. *Hastings Science and Technology Law Journal* 4(1): 159–207.

Grow, B., Cady, J., Rutledge, S. and Polek, D. (2006) Gold rush: online payments systems like e-gold Ltd. are becoming the currency of choice for cybercrooks. *Business Week*, 9 January.

Güring, P. and Grigg, I. (2011) Bitcoin and Gresham's Law – the economic inevitability of collapse. Mimeo. (http://iang.org/ papers/BitcoinBreachesGreshamsLaw.pdf)

Harper, J. (2013) It's just money. *The Digital Private Economy*, 8 July. (http://www.cato-unbound.org/2013/07/08/jim-harper/ its-just-money)

Hutchinson, M. (2013) Banking secrecy is a key civil liberty. *The Bear's Lair*, 29 April.

Lee, T. B. (2011) Bitcoin's collusion problem. (http://timothyblee. com/2011/04/19/bitcoins-collusion-problem/)

Matonis, J. (2012) WikiLeaks bypasses financial blockade with Bitcoin. *Forbes*, 20 August.

May, T. (1988) The crypto-anarchist manifesto. (http://invisible molotov.files.wordpress.com/2008/06/cryptoanarchist-mani festo.pdf)

Nakamoto, S. (2009) Bitcoin: a peer-to-peer electronic cash system. (http://bitcoin.org/bitcoin.pdf)

NotHaus, B. von (ed.) (2003) *The Liberty Dollar Solution to the Federal Reserve*. American Financial Press.

Paganini, P. (2013) How to profit illegally from Bitcoin ... cybercrime and much more. Infosec Institute Resources. (http:// resources.infosecinstitute.com/how-to-profit-illegally-from -bitcoin-cybercrime-and-much-more/)

Pratt, J. (2011) A free market standard: transitioning from a government fiat currency to a private, value-based, free-market money system based 100% on gold and silver. *Economic Research Paper* Serial no. 9, 16 November.

Rounds, B. (2011) Liberty Dollar II: did prosecutor Anne Tompkins violate ethics rules? (http://www.howtovanish.com/

2011/04/liberty-dollar-ii-prosecutor-anne-tompkins-made
-false-statement-of-law/)

Selgin, G. A. (2009) *Good Money: Birmingham Button Makers, the Royal Mint, and the Beginnings of Modern Coinage, 1775–1821.* University of Michigan Press.

Taylor A. J. P. (1965) *English History 1914–1965.* Oxford University Press.

Timberlake, R. H., Jr (1984) The central banking role of clearinghouse associations. *Journal of Money, Credit, and Banking* 17(1): 1–15.

Timberlake, R. H., Jr (1987) Private production of scrip money in the isolated community. *Journal of Money, Credit, and Banking* 19(4): 437–47.

US Attorney's Office, Western District of North Carolina (2011) Defendant convicted of minting his own currency. Press Release, 18 March. (http://www.fbi.gov/charlotte/press-releases/2011/defendant-convicted-of-minting-his-own-currency)

Wallace, B. (2011) The rise and fall of Bitcoin. *Wired*, December. (http://www.wired.com/magazine/2011/11/mf_bitcoin/)

White, L. H. (Forthcoming) What needs to be done to allow competition from alternative moneys? The case of the Liberty Dollar and e-gold. *Cato Journal.*

Zetter, K. (2009) Bullion and bandits: the improbable rise and fall of e-gold. *Wired*, 9 June. (http://www.wired.com/threatlevel/2009/06/e-gold/all/1)

ABOUT THE IEA

The Institute is a research and educational charity (No. CC 235 351), limited by guarantee. Its mission is to improve understanding of the fundamental institutions of a free society by analysing and expounding the role of markets in solving economic and social problems.

The IEA achieves its mission by:

- a high-quality publishing programme
- conferences, seminars, lectures and other events
- outreach to school and college students
- brokering media introductions and appearances

The IEA, which was established in 1955 by the late Sir Antony Fisher, is an educational charity, not a political organisation. It is independent of any political party or group and does not carry on activities intended to affect support for any political party or candidate in any election or referendum, or at any other time. It is financed by sales of publications, conference fees and voluntary donations.

In addition to its main series of publications the IEA also publishes a quarterly journal, *Economic Affairs*.

The IEA is aided in its work by a distinguished international Academic Advisory Council and an eminent panel of Honorary Fellows. Together with other academics, they review prospective IEA publications, their comments being passed on anonymously to authors. All IEA papers are therefore subject to the same rigorous independent refereeing process as used by leading academic journals.

IEA publications enjoy widespread classroom use and course adoptions in schools and universities. They are also sold throughout the world and often translated/reprinted.

Since 1974 the IEA has helped to create a worldwide network of 100 similar institutions in over 70 countries. They are all independent but share the IEA's mission.

Views expressed in the IEA's publications are those of the authors, not those of the Institute (which has no corporate view), its Managing Trustees, Academic Advisory Council members or senior staff.

Members of the Institute's Academic Advisory Council, Honorary Fellows, Trustees and Staff are listed on the following page.

The Institute gratefully acknowledges financial support for its publications programme and other work from a generous benefaction by the late Alec and Beryl Warren.

Other papers recently published by the IEA include:

Taxation and Red Tape
The Cost to British Business of Complying with the UK Tax System
Francis Chittenden, Hilary Foster & Brian Sloan
Research Monograph 64; ISBN 978-0-255-36612-0; £12.50

Ludwig von Mises – A Primer
Eamonn Butler
Occasional Paper 143; ISBN 978-0-255-36629-8; £7.50

Does Britain Need a Financial Regulator?
Statutory Regulation, Private Regulation and Financial Markets
Terry Arthur & Philip Booth
Hobart Paper 169; ISBN 978-0-255-36593-2; £12.50

Hayek's The Constitution of Liberty
An Account of Its Argument
Eugene F. Miller
Occasional Paper 144; ISBN 978-0-255-36637-3; £12.50

Fair Trade without the Froth
A Dispassionate Economic Analysis of 'Fair Trade'
Sushil Mohan
Hobart Paper 170; ISBN 978-0-255-36645-8; £10.00

A New Understanding of Poverty
Poverty Measurement and Policy Implications
Kristian Niemietz
Research Monograph 65; ISBN 978-0-255-36638-0; £12.50

The Challenge of Immigration
A Radical Solution
Gary S. Becker
Occasional Paper 145; ISBN 978-0-255-36613-7; £7.50

Sharper Axes, Lower Taxes
Big Steps to a Smaller State
Edited by Philip Booth
Hobart Paperback 38; ISBN 978-0-255-36648-9; £12.50

Self-employment, Small Firms and Enterprise
Peter Urwin
Research Monograph 66; ISBN 978-0-255-36610-6; £12.50

Crises of Governments
The Ongoing Global Financial Crisis and Recession
Robert Barro
Occasional Paper 146; ISBN 978-0-255-36657-1; £7.50

… and the Pursuit of Happiness
Wellbeing and the Role of Government
Edited by Philip Booth
Readings 64; ISBN 978-0-255-36656-4; £12.50

Public Choice – A Primer
Eamonn Butler
Occasional Paper 147; ISBN 978-0-255-36650-2; £10.00

The Profit Motive in Education: Continuing the Revolution
Edited by James B. Stanfield
Readings 65; ISBN 978-0-255-36646-5; £12.50

Which Road Ahead – Government or Market?
Oliver Knipping & Richard Wellings
Hobart Paper 171; ISBN 978-0-255-36619-9; £10.00

The Future of the Commons
Beyond Market Failure and Government Regulation
Elinor Ostrom et al.
Occasional Paper 148; ISBN 978-0-255-36653-3; £10.00

Redefining the Poverty Debate
Why a War on Markets Is No Substitute for a War on Poverty
Kristian Niemietz
Research Monograph 67; ISBN 978-0-255-36652-6; £12.50

The Euro – the Beginning, the Middle … and the End?
Edited by Philip Booth
Hobart Paperback 39; ISBN 978-0-255-36680-9; £12.50

The Shadow Economy
Friedrich Schneider & Colin C. Williams
Hobart Paper 172; ISBN 978-0-255-36674-8; £12.50

Quack Policy
Abusing Science in the Cause of Paternalism
Jamie Whyte
Hobart Paper 173; ISBN 978-0-255-36673-1; £10.00

Foundations of a Free Society
Eamonn Butler
Occasional Paper 149; ISBN 978-0-255-36687-8; £12.50

The Government Debt Iceberg
Jagadeesh Gokhale
Research Monograph 68; ISBN 978-0-255-36666-3; £10.00

A U-Turn on the Road to Serfdom
Grover Norquist
Occasional Paper 150; ISBN 978-0-255-36686-1; £10.00

Other IEA publications

Comprehensive information on other publications and the wider work of the IEA can be found at www.iea.org.uk. To order any publication please see below.

Personal customers

Orders from personal customers should be directed to the IEA:

Clare Rusbridge
IEA
2 Lord North Street
FREEPOST LON10168
London SW1P 3YZ
Tel: 020 7799 8907. Fax: 020 7799 2137
Email: sales@iea.org.uk

Trade customers

All orders from the book trade should be directed to the IEA's distributor:

NBN International (IEA Orders)
Orders Dept.
NBN International
10 Thornbury Road
Plymouth PL6 7PP
Tel: 01752 202301, Fax: 01752 202333
Email: orders@nbninternational.com

IEA subscriptions

The IEA also offers a subscription service to its publications. For a single annual payment (currently £42.00 in the UK), subscribers receive every monograph the IEA publishes. For more information please contact:

Clare Rusbridge
Subscriptions
IEA
2 Lord North Street
FREEPOST LON10168
London SW1P 3YZ
Tel: 020 7799 8907, Fax: 020 7799 2137
Email: crusbridge@iea.org.uk